Java

Paul Dixon

Credits

Footprint credits
Editor: Nicola Gibbs
Production and layout: Emma Bryers
Maps: Kevin Feeney

Managing Director: Andy Riddle
Commercial Director: Patrick Dawson
Publisher: Alan Murphy
Publishing Managers: Felicity Laughton,
Nicola Gibbs
Digital Editors: Jo Williams, Tom Mellors
Marketing and PR: Liz Harper
Sales: Diane McEntee
Advertising: Renu Sibal
Finance and Administration:
Elizabeth Taylor

Photography credits
Front cover: Manamana/Shutterstock
Back cover: Kirill Troponov/Shutterstock

Printed in Great Britain by CPI Antony Rowe,
Chippenham, Wiltshire

Every effort has been made to ensure that
the facts in this guidebook are accurate.
However, travellers should still obtain advice
from consulates, airlines, etc, about travel
and visa requirements before travelling.
The authors and publishers cannot accept
responsibility for any loss, injury or
inconvenience however caused.

Publishing information
Footprint *Focus Java*
1st edition
© Footprint Handbooks Ltd
November 2011

ISBN: 978 1 908206 44 2
CIP DATA: A catalogue record for this book
is available from the British Library

® Footprint Handbooks and the Footprint
mark are a registered trademark of
Footprint Handbooks Ltd

Published by Footprint
6 Riverside Court
Lower Bristol Road
Bath BA2 3DZ, UK
T +44 (0)1225 469141
F +44 (0)1225 469461
footprinttravelguides.com

Distributed in the USA by Globe Pequot
Press, Guilford, Connecticut

The content of Footprint *Focus Java*
has been taken directly from Footprint's
Southeast Asia Handbook which
was researched and written by
Andrew Spooner and Paul Dixon.

Contents

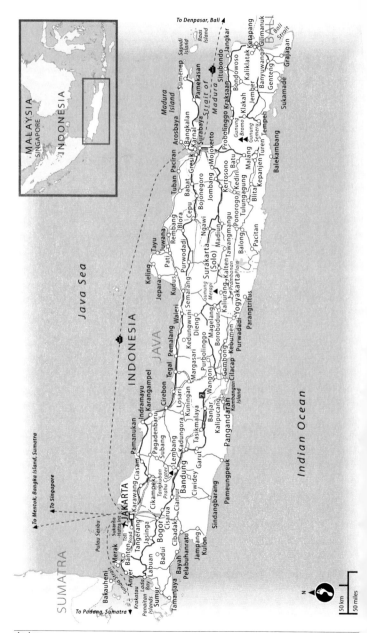

Java is Indonesia's political, economic and cultural heartland. With 60% of the country's population, the capital Jakarta, and the great bulk of Indonesia's industrial muscle, Java is the critical piece in the Indonesian jigsaw. It was here that many of the early, pre-colonial empires and kingdoms were based – reflected in monuments such as Borobudur and Prambanan, and in many smaller temples. Cities like Yogyakarta and Solo remain vibrant artistic and cultural centres, while Bogor and Bandung show more clearly the hand of the relatively short-lived Dutch presence. The latter, particularly, is renowned for its art deco architecture. Jakarta, as Indonesia's capital, has the most restaurants, the largest museums, and the widest array of shopping, but it is not a particularly enticing city.

The hand of humans has always had to contend with the forces of nature and nowhere is this clearer than in the battle against Java's volcanoes. From Krakatau off the west coast of Java to Gunung Bromo in East Java, a spine of active volcanoes runs through the island. While these volcanoes periodically bring destruction, they also provide the basis for a string of hill resorts and towns, and the fertile soil needed for feeding this incredibly densely populated island.

Planning your trip

Getting there

Jakarta's **Soekarno-Hatta Airport** ① *25 km northwest of the city, T021 550 5177, www. jakartasoekarnohattaairport.com,* is where most visitors arrive. It connects Jakarta with all other major cities and towns in the country, as well as regional and global destinations. Budget carriers flying into Jakarta include **AirAsia** (from Singapore, KL in Malaysia, Bangkok and Phuket in Thailand), and **Jetstar Asia** (from Singapore). State-owned **Garuda, Merpati** and all international airlines operate from Terminal 2. Domestic airlines use Terminal 1. Terminal 3 is used by **Indonesia AirAsia**.

Facilities at the airport include car rental, currency exchange booths, ATMs, left-luggage facilities (outside the Arrivals hall), hotel booking counter, a taxi desk, tourist information desk (with maps), the **Transit Hotel**, the **Transit Restaurant**, fast-food outlets, a 24-hour post office, long-distance calls, and internet and cell phone connectivity facilities.

Metered taxis to the centre of town cost about 90,000Rp (plus toll fees of 11,500Rp). Only taxis with official Taxi Bandara stickers on their windscreens are allowed to pick up passengers at the airport. The airport authorities hand out complaints cards for visitors to complete, setting out the toll charges and surcharges applicable. Allow at least an hour to reach the airport from the centre of town, more at peak times. **Damri** ① *T021 550 1290, www.damri.co.id,* runs air-conditioned buses from Terminal 2 F/E to Jakarta's Gambir railway station every 15-30 minutes from 0500-1830 (one hour, 20,000Rp).

The **Gambir railway station** is also a major arrival point in Jakarta. There is a **Blue Bird** taxi rank just to the north of the station, which charges a 4500Rp surcharge. The journey to Jalan Jaksa costs around 20,000Rp (the centre for budget accommodation). Alternatively, those with little luggage will be able to manage the 10-minute walk. Air-conditioned Damri buses also run to Blok M, Jalan Bulungan, and Kemayoran. There are also buses running to Bogor (35,000Rp) and Bandung (70,000Rp), for those that want to avoid Jakarta. Many of the first-class hotels lay on transport.

Getting around

Air

The most convenient and comfortable way to travel is by air. **Garuda** (www.garuda-indonesia. com) and **Merpati** (www.merpati.co.id) service all the main provincial cities. Merpati tends to operate the short-hop services to smaller destinations, particularly in eastern Indonesia.

The other main domestic airlines are **Lion Air** (www.lionair.co.id), proud owner of a fleet of sparkling B737-900s, and **Indonesia AirAsia** (www.airasia.com). Other key players are **Batavia Air** (www.batavia-air.co.id) and **Sriwijaya** (www.sriwijayaair-online.com). All these airlines cover major destinations in Indonesia. Smallest of all are **DAS, SMAC** and **Deraya** (www.deraya.co.id) and **Susi Air** (www.susiair.com), which tend to service smaller towns in Java and the outer islands, especially Kalimantan and Sumatra. In Nusa Tenggara, travellers often have to use Merpati, or one of the local outfits such as **Trans Nusa** (www.transnusa. co.id) and **Indonesia Air Transport** (www.iat.co.id).

By international standards, flights in Indonesia are cheap. It is also considerably cheaper buying tickets in Indonesia than it is purchasing them abroad. Airlines such as Garuda, Lion

Air, Batavia Air and AirAsia have an online booking system for use with Visa or MasterCard. Garuda flights can be reserved online. Offices in larger towns will usually accept credit card payment, although smaller branch offices in out-of-the-way places will often only take cash payment. Some airlines give student reductions. During holiday periods, flights are booked up some time ahead. ▸▸ *For details of domestic airport tax, see page 19.*

Boat
The national shipping company is **Pelayaran Nasional Indonesia (PELNI)** ① *Jln Gajah Mada 14, Jakarta, T021 633 4342, www.pelni.co.id*. Many travel agents also sell PELNI tickets and, although they levy a small surcharge, may be far more convenient. PELNI operates a fleet of modern passenger ships that ply fortnightly circuits throughout the archipelago. The ships are well run and well maintained, have an excellent safety record, and are a comfortable and leisurely way to travel. Each accommodates 500-2250 passengers in five classes, has central air conditioning, a bar, restaurant and cafeteria. The unprecedented growth in the domestic airline industry in the past few years has seen PELNI profits take a beating, with more and more routes being cut annually. Note that sailing with PELNI can take some planning as departures in more remote parts of the country can be as far apart as two weeks. Check the PELNI website for the lastest schedule.

Rail
Passenger train services are limited to Java and certain areas of Sumatra. Trains are usually slow and often delayed. Single track connects many major cities. First class is air conditioned with a dining car. There are two main trunk routes on Java: Jakarta–Cirebon–Semarang–Surabaya and Jakarta–Bandung–Yogyakarta–Solo (Surakarta)–Surabaya. The principal services are identified by name, for example, the *Bima* is the air-conditioned night-express from Jakarta via Yogya and Solo, to Surabaya (12 hours); the *Mutiara Utara* is the northern route train to Surabaya via Semarang; the *Senja Utama Solo* is the express train to Yogya and Solo; while the *Senja Utama Semarang* is the express train to Cirebon and Semarang. There are three classes: **Eksekutif** is first class, with air conditioning, reclining seats and breakfast included. **Business** (*bisnis*) is fan-cooled, with pillows provided; and **Ekonomi**, with rather run-down, well-used coaches, broken fans and windows that may or may not open – this class is subject to overcrowding. All three classes can be booked. Reservations should be made well in advance; it is often easier through a travel agent in the town where you are staying. Fares and timetables can be found at www.kereta-api.co.id (only in Indonesian) – for schedules, train names and fares head to the 'Jadwal & Tarif' link.

Road
Bicycle In some of the more popular tourist destinations, guesthouses and some tour companies hire out bicycles. These vary in quality – check the brakes before you set off. Expect to pay about 25,000Rp per day for a locally or Chinese-built mountain bike.

Bus Road transport in Indonesia has improved greatly in recent years, and main roads on most of the islands are generally in reasonably good condition though somewhat overcrowded. In many areas main roads may be impassable during the rainy season and after severe storms.

Most Indonesians get around by bus. The network is vast and although it is not always quick or comfortable, buses are the cheapest way to travel. There are a range of bus alternatives from **Bis Ekonomi** (dirt cheap, cramped but a good way to mingle with Indonesians), to **Bis VIP** (icy cold, fully reclinable seats with plenty of space). Visitors are most likely to find themselves on fairly comfy **Bis Malam**, air-conditioned buses that plough the roads of the archipelago each night and deposit red-eyed passengers at their desination at dawn just in time for morning prayers.

Avoid the seats at the front, which are the most dangerous if there is a crash. Roads are often windy and rough, and buses are badly sprung (or totally un-sprung). Despite harrowingly fast speeds at times, do not expect to average much more than 40 kph except on the best highways. Overnight buses are usually faster and recommended for longer journeys. However, air-conditioned overnighters can be very cold and a sarong or blanket is useful.

Tickets can be obtained from bus company offices or through travel agents; shop around for the best fare – bargaining is possible. It is sensible to book a day or so ahead for longer journeys. During Ramadan and at Lebaran, all forms of public transport are packed.

Shuttle buses or **Travels** are found in the main tourist areas on Bali and Lombok and increasingly between the major cities in Java. In Bali they operate almost exclusively for the benefit of foreigners connecting the most popular destinations, with a fixed daily timetable. They will pick up and drop off passengers at their hotels and take a great deal of the hassle out of travel.

Car and motorbike hire   Cars can be hired for self-drive or with a driver. Motorbike hire is available at many beach resorts and increasingly in other towns. It is illegal to ride without a helmet, although this can just be a construction worker's hard hat. Many machines are poorly maintained: check brakes and lights before paying.

Taxi   Taxis are metered in the major cities. Drivers often cannot change large bills. All registered taxis, minibuses and rental cars have yellow number plates; black number plates are for private vehicles, and red are for government-owned vehicles.

Other forms of local road transport

Bajaj   Small three-wheeled motor scooters similar to the Thai tuk-tuk. They are probably the cheapest form of 'taxi' after the becak, but are only available in big cities.

Becaks   Becaks or bicycle rickshaws are one of the cheapest, and most important, forms of short-distance transport in Indonesia. Literally hundreds of thousands of poor people make a living driving becaks. However, they are now illegal in central Jakarta and often officially barred from main thoroughfares in other large cities. Bargain hard and agree a fare before boarding.

Bemos   These are small buses or adapted pickups operating on fixed routes. They usually run fixed routes for fixed fares (it varies between towns, but around 3000Rp), can also be chartered by the hour or day.

Ojeks   Motorcycle taxis. Ojek riders, often wearing coloured jackets, congregate at junctions, taking passengers pillion to their destination. Agree a price before boarding and bargain hard.

Oplets   Larger versions of bemos carrying 10-12 passengers. They have a bewildering number of other names – daihatsu in Semarang, angkuta in Solo, microlets in Jakarta, while in rural areas they tend to be called colts. In larger cities, bemos/colts often follow fixed routes. They are sometimes colour coded, sometimes numbered, sometimes have their destinations marked on the front – and sometimes all three. For intra-city trips there is usually a fixed fare (it varies between towns, but around 3000Rp) although it is worth asking one of your fellow passengers what the *harga biasa* (normal price) is, or watch what is being handed to the driver or his sidekick by fellow passengers. In the countryside, routes can vary and so do fares; be prepared to bargain. Oplets can also be chartered by the hour or day (bargain hard).

Sleeping and eating price codes

$$$$ over US$100   **$$$** US$46-100
$$ US$21-45   **$**   US$20 and under
Price codes refer to the cost of a standard double/twin room in high season.

$$$ over US$12   **$$** US$6-12   **$** under US$6
Price codes refer to the cost of a two-course meal, not including drinks.

Maps
Locally, maps may not be available beyond the larger cities, and often the quality is poor.
Nelles A good series of maps of the major islands and island groups.
Periplus Travel Maps A recent series of maps to the major islands including some to individual provinces. Good on tourist site information and often with good city insets.

Sleeping → *For hotel price codes, see box, above.*

Tourist and business centres usually have a good range of accommodation for all budgets. Bali, for example, has some of the finest hotels in the world – at a corresponding price – along with excellent mid- and lower-range accommodation. However, visitors venturing off the beaten track may find hotels restricted to dingy and over-priced establishments catering for local businessmen and officials. The best-run and most competitively priced budget accommodation is found in popular tourist spots – like Bali and Yogya. It is almost always worth bargaining. This is particularly true for hotels in tourist destinations that attract a fair amount of local weekend business: the weekday room rate may be 50% less than the weekend rate. All hotels are required to display their room rates (for every category of room) on a *daftar harga*, or price list. This is invariably either in public view in the reception area or will be produced when you ask about room rates. Indonesians prefer to be on the ground floor, so rooms on higher floors are usually cheaper. In cheaper accommodation, the bed may consist only of a bottom sheet and pillow with no top sheet.

Terminology can be confusing: a *losmen* is a lower price range hotel (in parts of Sumatra and in some other areas, *losmen* are known as *penginapan*); a *wisma* is a guesthouse, but these can range in price from cheap to moderately expensive; finally, a *hotel* is a hotel, but can range from the cheap and squalid up to a Hilton.

With the economy faring well in Indonesia in recent years, and a more affluent middle class emerging, mid-range and top-end hotels are being built at an extraordinary rate, many offering excellent promotion rates and possessing all the mod cons an international traveller requires. The backpacker market has seen less money being poured into it than, for example, in Malaysia and Thailand, and these places can often seem to be a bit bleak and tawdry compared to cheaper digs elsewhere in Southeast Asia. The exception to this is in Bali and some parts of Lombok, where the backpacker market is still pulling in the rupiah and there are a few gems to be found.

Bathing and toilets
Baths and showers are not a feature of many cheaper *losmen*. Instead a *mandi* (a water tank and ladle) is used to wash. The tub is not climbed into; water is ladled from the tub and

splashed over the head. The traditional Asian toilet is of the squat variety. (Toilets are called *kamar kecil* – the universal 'small room' – or *way say*, as in the initials 'WC'.) Toilet paper is not traditionally used; the faithful left hand and water suffice. In cheaper accommodation you are expected to bring your own towels, soap and toilet paper.

Eating and drinking → *For restaurant price codes, see box on previous page.*

Food

The main staple across the archipelago is rice. Today, alternatives such as corn, sweet potatoes and sago, which are grown primarily in the dry islands of the East, are regarded as 'poor man's food', and rice is the preferred staple.

Indonesians will eat rice – or *nasi* (milled, cooked rice) – at least three times a day. Breakfast is often left-over rice, stir-fried and served up as *nasi goreng*. Mid-morning snacks are often sticky rice cakes or *pisang goreng* (fried bananas). Rice is the staple for lunch, served up with two or three meat and vegetable dishes and followed by fresh fruit. The main meal is supper, which is served quite early and again consists of rice, this time accompanied by as many as five or six other dishes. *Sate/satay* (grilled skewers of meat), *soto* (a nourishing soup) or *bakmi* (noodles, a dish of Chinese origin) may be served first.

In many towns (particularly in Java), *sate*, *soto* or *bakmi* vendors roam the streets with carts containing charcoal braziers, ringing a bell or hitting a block (the noise will signify what he or she is selling) in the early evenings. These carts are known as *kaki lima* (five legs). *Pedagang* (vendor) *kaki lima* also refers to hawkers who peddle their wares from stalls and from baskets hung from shoulder poles.

Larger foodstalls tend to set up in the same place every evening in a central position in town. These *warungs*, as they are known, may be temporary structures or more permanent buildings, with simple tables and benches. In the larger cities, there may be an area of *warungs*, all under one roof. Often a particular street will become known as the best place to find particular dishes like *martabak* (savoury meat pancakes) or *gado gado* (vegetable salad served with peanut sauce). It is common to see some *warungs* labelled *wartegs*. These are stalls selling dishes from Tegal, a town on Java's north coast. More formalized restaurants are known simply as *rumah makan* (literally 'eating houses'), often shortened to just 'RM'. A good place to look for cheap stall food is in and around the market or *pasar*; night markets or *pasar malam* are usually better for eating than day markets.

Feast days, such as Lebaran marking the end of Ramadan, are a cause for great celebration and traditional dishes are served. *Lontong* or *ketupat* are made at this time (they are both versions of boiled rice – simmered in a small container or bag, so that as it cooks, the rice is compressed to make a solid block). This may be accompanied by *sambal goreng daging* (fried beef in a coconut sauce) in Java or *rendang* (curried beef) in Sumatra. *Nasi kuning* (yellow rice) is traditionally served at a *selamatan* (a Javanese celebration marking a birth, the collection of the rice harvest or the completion of a new house).

In addition to rice, there are a number of other common ingredients used across the country. Coconut milk, ginger, chilli peppers and peanuts are used nationwide, while dried salted fish and soybeans are important sources of protein. In coastal areas, fish and seafood tend to be more important than meat. As Indonesia is more than 80% Muslim, pork is not widely eaten (except in Chinese restaurants) but in some areas, such as Bali, Christian Flores and around Lake Toba in Sumatra, it is much more in evidence.

Regional cuisines

Although Indonesia is becoming more homogeneous as Javanese culture spreads to the Outer Islands, there are still distinctive regional cuisines. The food of Java embraces a number of regional forms, of which the most distinctive is **Sundanese**. *Lalap*, a Sundanese dish, consists of raw vegetables and is said to be the only Indonesian dish where vegetables are eaten uncooked. Characteristic ingredients of Javanese dishes are soybeans, beef, chicken and vegetables; characteristic flavours are an interplay of sweetness and spiciness. Probably the most famous regional cuisine, however, is **Padang** or **Minang** food, which has its origins in West Sumatra province. Padang food has 'colonized' the rest of the country and there are Padang restaurants in every town, no matter how small. Dishes tend to be hot and spicy, using quantities of chilli and turmeric, and include *rendang* (dry beef curry), *kalo ayam* (creamy chicken curry) and *dendeng balado* (fried seasoned sun-dried meat with a spicy coating). In **Eastern Indonesia**, seafood and fish are important elements in the diet, and fish grilled over an open brazier (*ikan panggang* or *ikan bakar*) and served with spices and rice is a delicious, common dish. The **Toraja** of Sulawesi eat large amounts of pork, and specialities include black rice (*nasi hitam*) and fish or chicken cooked in bamboo (*piong*). There are large numbers of Chinese people scattered across the archipelago and, like other countries of the region, **Chinese** restaurants are widespread.

Drink

Water must be boiled for at least five minutes before it is safe to drink. Hotels and most restaurants should boil the water they offer customers. Ask for *air minum* (drinking water). Many restaurants provide a big jug of boiled water on each table. In cheaper establishments it is probably best to play safe and ask for bottled water, although consider the environmental impact of this.

'**Mineral water**' – of which the most famous is *Aqua* ('aqua' has become the generic word for mineral water) – is available in all but the smallest and most remote towns. Check the seal is intact before accepting a bottle. Bottled water is cheap: in 2011 a 1.5 litre bottle cost around 3500Rp. Bottled water is considerably cheaper at supermarkets than at the many kiosks lining the streets.

Western **bottled and canned drinks** are widely available in Indonesia and are comparatively cheap. Alternatively, most restaurants will serve *air jeruk* (citrus **fruit juices**) with or without ice (*es*). The **coconut milk** is a good thirst quencher and a good source of potassium and glucose. Fresh fruit juices vary greatly in quality; some are little more than water, sugar and ice. Ice in many places is fine, but in cheaper restaurants and away from tourist areas many people recommend taking drinks without ice. Javanese, Sumatran, Sulawesi or Timorese *kopi* (coffee), fresh and strong, is an excellent morning pick-you-up. It is usually served *kopi manis* (sweet) and black; if you want to have it without sugar, ask for it *tidak pakai gula*. The same goes for other drinks habitually served with mountains of sugar (like fruit juices). *Susu* (milk) is available in tourist areas and large towns, but it may be sweetened condensed milk. *Teh* (tea), usually weak, is obtainable almost everywhere. *Teh jahe* (hot ginger tea) is a refreshing alternative.

Although Indonesia is a predominantly Muslim country, alcohol is widely available. The two most popular **beers** – light lagers – are the locally brewed *Anker* and *Bintang* brands. Wine is becoming more popular. A reasonable bottle can be had for around US$15. Imported **spirits** are comparatively expensive, however, a number of local brews including *brem* (rice wine), *arak* (rice whisky) and *tuak* (palm wine) are available.

Local customs and laws

As a rule, Indonesians are courteous and understanding. Visitors should be the same. Foreigners are often given the benefit of the doubt when norms are transgressed. However, it is best to have a grasp of at least the basics of accepted behaviour. There are also some areas – such as Aceh in North Sumatra – that are more fervently Muslim than other parts of the country. With such a diverse array of cultures and religions, accepted conduct varies. Generally, the more popular an area is (as a tourist destination) the more understanding local people are likely to be of tourist habits. But this is not to imply that anything goes. It is also true that familiarity can breed contempt, so even in places like Bali it is important to be sensitive to the essentials of local culture.

Calmness Like other countries of Southeast Asia, a calm attitude is highly admired, especially if things are going wrong. Keep calm and cool when bargaining, or waiting for a delayed bus or appointment.

Dress Indonesia is largely a Muslim country. Dress modestly and avoid shorts, short skirts and sleeveless dresses or shirts (except at the beach). Public nudity and topless bathing are not acceptable. Light clothing is suitable all year round, except at night in the mountains. Proper decorum should be observed when visiting places of worship; shorts are not permitted in mosques, shoulders and arms should be covered, and women must cover their heads. Formal dress for men normally consists of a batik shirt and trousers; suits are rarely worn. Local women usually wear a *kebaya*.

Face People should not be forced to lose face in public; especially in front of colleagues. Putting someone in a position of *malu* or social shame should be avoided.

Gifts If you are invited to somebody's home, it is customary to take a gift. This is not opened until after the visitor has left. Most small general stores have a range of pre-wrapped and boxed gifts, appropriate for a variety of occasions including weddings. These are usually items of china or glasses.

Heads, hands and feet The head is considered sacred and should never be touched (especially those of children). Handshaking is common among both men and women, but the use of the left hand to give or receive is taboo. When eating with fingers, use the right hand only. Pointing with your finger is impolite; use your thumb to point. Beckon buses (or any person) with a flapping motion of your right hand down by your side. When sitting with others, do not cross your legs; it is considered disrespectful. Do not point with your feet and keep them off tables. Remove shoes when entering houses.

Open affection Public displays of affection between men and women are considered objectionable. However, Indonesians of the same sex tend to be affectionate – holding hands, for example.

Punctuality *Jam karet* or 'rubber time' is a peculiarly Indonesian phenomenon. Patience and a cool head are very important; appointments are rarely at the time arranged.

Religion Indonesia is the largest Muslim country in the world. In Java, **Islam** is a synthesis of Islam, Buddhism, Hinduism and Animism – although the extent to which it is 'syncretic' is vigorously debated. Orthodox Islam is strongest in northern Sumatra, but is also present in parts of Sulawesi, Kalimantan and West Java. Since the Bali bombings and suicide attacks in Jakarta, Islam in Indonesia, and the *pesentren* (Islamic boarding schools – the most famous being Al-Mukmin Ngruki in Java with graduates including the Bali bombers) have been put under the microscope with the government keen to disassociate itself with any links to fundamentalist groups. However, the government has so far proved itself unable to stop radical groups agitating, despite placing huge emphasis on intelligence and anti-terror schemes.

Mosques are sacred houses of prayer; non-Muslims can enter a mosque, so long as they observe the appropriate customs: remove shoes before entering, dress appropriately, do not disturb the peace, and do not walk too close to or in front of somebody who is praying. During the fasting month of Ramadan, do not eat, drink or smoke in the presence of Muslims during daylight hours.

Bali has remained a **Hindu** island, and remnants of Hinduism are also evident in parts of Central and East Java. To enter a temple or *pura* on Bali, it is often necessary to wear a sash around the waist (at some temples a sarong is also required); these are available for hire at the more popular temples, or can be bought for about 10,000Rp (20,000Rp for a sarong). Modest and tidy dress is also required when visiting Hindu temples; women should not enter wearing short dresses or with bare shoulders. Do not use flash during ceremonies. Women menstruating are requested not to enter temples.

Pockets of **Christianity** can be found throughout the archipelago, notably in East Nusa Tenggara, around Danau Toba and Sulawesi. Evangelical Christianity is enjoying large numbers of converts among the ethnic Chinese.

Indonesian festivals and events → *Muslim festivals are based on the lunar calendar.*

January
Tahun Baru, New Year's Day (1st: public holiday). **New Year's Eve** is celebrated with street carnivals, shows, fireworks and all-night festivities. In Christian areas, festivities are more exuberant, with people visiting each other on New Year's Day and attending church services.

January/February
Imlek, Chinese New Year (movable, 23 Jan 2012, 10 Feb 2013). An official holiday; many Chinese shops and businesses close for at least 2 days. Within the Chinese community, younger people visit their relatives, children are given *hong bao* (lucky money), new clothes are bought and any unfinished business is cleared up.

March/April
Garebeg Maulad, or Maulud Nabi Muhammed, birthday of the Prophet Mohammad, (movable, 4 Feb 2012, 24 Jan 2013: public holiday), to commemorate Prophet Muhammad's birthday in AD 571. Processions and Koran recitals in most big towns. Celebrations begin a week before the actual day and last a month, with *selamatans* in homes, mosques and schools.

Wafat Isa Al-Masih, Good Friday (movable, 6 Apr 2012, 29 March 2013: public holiday). **Nyepi** (movable, 23 Mar 2012, 06 April 2013: public holiday). Solar New Year, which is held at the spring equinox. In the recent past it was a day of silence when everything closed down and no activity was allowed. It is hoped that the evil spirits roused by the previous night's activities will find Bali to be a barren land and will leave the island. On the day before Nyepi long parades of traditionally dressed Balinese, carrying offerings and sacred objects, walk from their villages to nearby riverbanks and beaches to undertake ritual ablutions of purification and ask for their deity's blessing. As part of the *melasti* rites, the village gods in their *pratimas* (the small statue in which a god is invited to reside during a ceremony) are taken from the village temples and carried to the seashore for resanctification. Balinese believe that the sea will receive all evil and polluted elements, it is a place to cast off the evil words and deeds of the past year, and seek renewal and purification for the new Hindu year.

Note Visitors must stay within their hotel compounds from 0500 to 0500 the following day; the observance of Nyepi is very strict in this regard, you might choose to avoid being on the island during this time. Tourists are confined to their accommodation, which in a small guesthouse means you feel as if you have been placed under 'house arrest' – no swimming in the sea 10 m from your bungalow, no strolls or other forms of exercise. Anyone arriving at Denpasar airport on the eve of Nyepi should be aware that most taxi drivers go home at 1700. The few who continue to offer a taxi service up to midnight ask exorbitant rates and may be unlicensed. Travellers should arrange transport in advance with their accommodation.

Kartini Day (21 Apr). A ceremony held by women to mark the birthday of Raden Ajeng Kartini, born in 1879 and proclaimed as a pioneer of women's emancipation. Women are supposed to be pampered by their husbands and children, although it is women's organizations like the Dharma Wanita who get most excited. Women wear national dress.

May

Waisak Day (movable, 28 Apr 2012, 25 May 2013: public holiday). Marks the birth and death of the historic Buddha; at Candi Mendut outside Yogyakarta, a procession of monks carrying flowers, candles, holy fire and images of the Buddha walk to Borobudur.
Kenaikan Isa Al-Masih or Ascension Day (movable, 17 May 2012, 9 May 2013: public holiday).

June/July

Al Miraj or Isra Miraj Nabi Muhammed (movable, 16 Jun 2012, 5 Jun 2013). The ascension of the Prophet Mohammad when he is led through the 7 heavens by the archangel. He speaks with God and returns to earth the same night, with instructions that include the 5 daily prayers.

August

Independence Day (17 Aug: public holiday). The most important national holiday, celebrated with processions and dancing.

Although it's officially on 17 Aug, festivities continue for a month, towns are decorated with bunting and parades cause delays to bus travel, there seems to be no way of knowing when each town will hold its parades.
Awal Ramadan (movable, 19 Jul 2012, 9 Jul 2013). The 1st day of Ramadan, a month of fasting for all Muslims. Muslims abstain from all food, drink and smoking from sunrise to sundown – if they are very strict, Muslims do not even swallow their own saliva during daylight hours. It is strictly adhered to in more conservative areas like Aceh and West Sumatra, and many restaurants remain closed during daylight hours – making life tiresome for non-Muslims. Every evening for 30 days before breaking of fast, stalls selling traditional Malay cakes and delicacies are set up. The only people exempt from fasting are the elderly, those who are travelling and women who are pregnant or menstruating.

September

Idul Fitri (Aidil Fitri) or **Lebaran** (movable, 18 Aug 2012, 9 Aug 2013: public holiday) is a 2-day celebration that marks the end of Ramadan, and is a period of prayer and celebration. In order for Hari Raya to be declared, the new moon of Syawal has to be sighted; if it is not, fasting continues for another day. It is the most important time of the year for Muslim families. Mass prayers are held in mosques and squares. Public transport is booked up weeks in advance and hotels are often full.

October

Hari Pancasila (1 Oct). This commemorates the Five Basic Principles of Pancasila.
Armed Forces Day (5 Oct). The anniversary of the founding of the Indonesian Armed Forces; military parades and demonstrations.

November/December

Idhul Adha (movable, 25 Oct 2012, 15 Oct 2013: public holiday). Celebrated by

Muslims to mark the 10th day of Zulhijjah, the 12th month of the Islamic calendar when pilgrims celebrate their return from the Haj to Mecca. In the morning, prayers are offered; later, families hold 'open house'. This is the 'festival of the sacrifice'. Burial graves are cleaned, and an animal is sacrificed to be distributed to the poor to commemorate the willingness of Abraham to sacrifice his son. Indonesian men who have made the pilgrimage to Mecca wear a white skull-hat.

Muharram (movable, 14 Nov 2012, 4 Nov 2013: public holiday), Muslim New Year. Marks the 1st day of the Muslim calendar and celebrates the Prophet Muhammad's journey from Mecca to Medina on the lunar equivalent of AD 16 Jul 622.

Christmas Day (25 Dec: public holiday). Celebrated by Christians – the Bataks of Sumatra, the Toraja and Minahasans of Sulawesi and in some of the islands of Nusa Tenggara, and Irian Jaya.

Shopping

Indonesia offers a wealth of distinctive handicrafts and other products. Best buys include textiles (batik and *ikat*), silverwork, woodcarving, *krisses* (indigenous daggers), puppets, paintings and ceramics. Bali has the greatest choice of handicrafts. It is not necessarily the case that you will find the best buys in the area where a particular product is made; the larger cities, especially Jakarta, sell a wide range of handicrafts and antiques from across the archipelago at competitive prices.

Tips on buying
Early morning sales may well be cheaper, as salespeople often believe the first sale augurs well for the rest of the day. Except in the larger fixed-price stores, bargaining (with good humour) is expected; start at 60% lower than the asking price. Do not expect to achieve instant results; if you walk away from the shop, you will almost certainly be followed, with a lower offer. If the salesperson agrees to your price, you should feel obliged to purchase – it is considered very ill mannered to agree on a price and then not buy the article.

What to buy
Centres of batik-making are focused on Java. Yogyakarta and Solo (Surakarta) probably offer the widest choice. There is also a good range of batik in Jakarta. The traditional hand-drawn batiks (*batik tulis*) are more expensive than the modern printed batiks. *Ikat* is dyed and woven cloth found on the islands of Bali, Lombok and Nusa Tenggara, although it is not cheap and is sometimes of dubious quality. *Wayang* is a Javanese and Balinese art form and puppets are most widely available on these islands, particularly in Yogyakarta and Jakarta. Baskets of all shapes and sizes are made for practical use, out of rattan, bamboo, sisal, and nipah and lontar palm. The intricate baskets of Lombok are particularly attractive. Woodcarving ranges from the clearly tourist oriented (Bali), to fine classical pieces (Java), to 'primitive' (Papua). The greatest concentration of woodcarvers work in Bali, producing skilful modern and traditional designs. For a more contemporary take on Indonesian fashion, head to the *distros* of Bandung (see page 56) for some seriously unique T-shirts and accessories.

Essentials A-Z

Accident and emergency
Ambulance T118, Fire T113, Police T110.

Customs and duty free
The duty-free allowance is 2 litres of alcohol, 200 cigarettes or 50 cigars or 100 g of tobacco, along with a reasonable amount of perfume.

Prohibited items include narcotics, arms and ammunition, pornographic objects or printed matter.

Internet
Any town of any size will have an internet café. Costs vary from 3000Rp-20,000Rp per hr. Indonesia is a surpisingly well-wired country and many hotels, cafés and even convenience stores offer Wi-Fi (though frustratingly hotels often charge for access). Smartphones, particulalarly Blackberry and their BBM (Blackberry messenger service) have taken off here in recent years.

Health
See your doctor or travel clinic at least 6 weeks before your departure for general advice on travel risks, malaria and vaccinations required for the region you are visiting. Make sure you have travel insurance, get a dental check (especially if you are going to be away for more than a month), know your own blood group and if you suffer a long-term condition such as diabetes or epilepsy make sure someone knows or that you have a Medic Alert bracelet/necklace with this information on it.

Health risks
The following covers some of the more common risks to travellers but is by no means comprehensive.

Malaria exists across the region. Always check with your doctor or travel clinic for the most up-to-date advice. Note that medicine in developing countries, in particular anti- malarials, may be sub-standard or part of a trade in counterfeit drugs. Malaria can cause death within 24 hrs. It can start as something resembling an attack of flu. You may feel tired, lethargic, headachy, feverish; or more seriously, develop fits, followed by coma and then death. Have a low index of suspicion because it is very easy to write off vague symptoms that may actually be malaria. If you have a temperature, go to a doctor as soon as you can and ask for a malaria test. On your return home if you suffer any of these symptoms, get tested as soon as possible, even if any previous test proved negative; a test could save your life.

The most serious viral disease is **dengue fever**, which is hard to protect against as the mosquitoes bite throughout the day as well as at night – use insect avoidance methods at all times. Symptoms are similar to malaria and include fever, intense joint pain and a rash. Rest, plenty of fluids and paracetamol is the best treatment.

Each year there is the possibility that **avian flu SARS** might rear their ugly heads. Check the news reports. If there is a problem in an area you are due to visit you may be advised to have an ordinary flu shot or to seek expert advice.

Rabies and **schistosomiasis** (bilharzia, a water-borne parasite) may be a problem. Be aware of the dangers of the bite from any animal. If bitten clean the wound and treat with an iodine-based disinfectant or alcohol. Always seek urgent medical attention even if you have been previously vaccinated.

Bites and stings are rare but if you are bitten by a snake, spider or scorpion, stay as calm as possible, try to identify the culprit and seek medical advice without delay.

Bacterial diseases include **tuberculosis** (TB) and some causes of traveller's diarrhoea. **Diarrhoea** is common but if symptoms persist beyond 2 weeks medical attention should be sought. Also seek medical advice if there is blood in the stools and/or fever. Keep well hydrated (rehydration sachets are invaluable) and eat bland foods. Bacterial diarrhoea is the most common; your GP may prescribe antibiotics for you to take with you. To minimize the chances of diarrhoea be careful with water (see below) and food, particularly salads, meat and unpasteurized dairy products. Where possible, watch food being prepared. There is a simple adage that says: wash it, peel it, boil it or forget it.

Typhoid is spread by the insanitary preparation of food. A number of vaccines are available, including one taken orally.

Water should be treated with iodine and filtered. Avoid tap water and ice in drinks. Check seals on bottled water are unbroken.

Take good heed of advice regarding protecting yourself against the sun. Overexposure can lead to **sunburn** and, in the longer term, skin cancers and premature skin aging. Avoid exposure to the sun by covering exposed skin, wearing a hat and staying out of the sun, particularly between late morning and early afternoon. Apply a high-factor sunscreen and also make sure it screens against UVB. A further danger in tropical climates is **heat exhaustion** or more seriously **heatstroke**. This can be avoided by good hydration, which means drinking water past the point of simply quenching thirst. Also when first exposed to tropical heat take time to acclimatize by avoiding strenuous activity in the middle of the day. If you cannot avoid heavy exercise it is also a good idea to increase salt intake.

Useful resources
www.btha.org British Travel Health Association (UK). This is the official website of an organization of travel health professionals.

www.cdc.gov US Government site that gives excellent advice on travel health and details of disease outbreaks.
www.fco.gov.uk Foreign and Commonwealth Office.
www.fitfortravel.scot.nhs.uk A-Z of vaccine/health advice for each country.
www.nathnac.org National Travel Health Network and Centre.
www.who.int The WHO Blue Book lists the diseases of the world.

Vaccinations See you doctor or a specialist travel clinic 6-8 weeks before travel for advice. The following vaccinations are usually advised before travel to Southeast Asia: BCG, diphtheria, hepatitis A, polio, tetanus and typhoid. The following are sometimes advised before travel to Southeast Asia: hepatitis B, Japanese B encephalitis, tuberculosis and rabies. A yellow fever vaccination certificate is required if coming from areas with risk of transmission. If you have been travelling in Africa or South America in a country in the yellow-fever zone within 6 days of arriving in Southeast Asia check to see if you require proof of vaccination.

Language
The national language is Bahasa Indonesia, which is written in Roman script. There are 250 regional languages and dialects, of which Sundanese (the language of West Java and Jakarta) is the most widespread. In Padang and elsewhere in West Sumatra, the population speak Minang, which is also similar to Bahasa. About 70% of the population can speak Bahasa. English is the most common foreign language, with some Dutch and Portuguese speakers.

Bahasa Indonesia is relatively easy to learn, a small number of useful words and phrases are listed in the box, above.

The best way to learn Indonesian is to study it intensively in Indonesia. In Jakarta and Bali, a variety of short and long courses (including homestay programmes in Bali) are available through **The Indonesia-Australia Language Foundation (IALF)**, T021 521 3350, www.ialf.edu. In Yogyakarta, another centre where overseas students study Indonesian, courses are run by the **Realia Language School**, T0274 583229, www.realians.com, which is recommended. It is cheaper if a group learns together.

Money → *US$1 = 8836Rp, £1 = 13,940Rp, €1 = 12,197Rp (Oct 2011)*

The unit of currency in Indonesia is the rupiah (Rp). When taking US$ in cash, make sure the bills are new and crisp, as banks in Indonesia can be fussy about which bills they accept (Flores and Sumatra are particularly bad). Larger denomination US$ bills also tend to command a premium exchange rate. In more out of the way places it is worth making sure that you have a stock of smaller notes and coins – it can be hard to break larger bills.

Two of the better banks are **Bank Negara Indonesia (BNI)** and **Bank Central Asia (BCA)**. BNI is reliable and efficient and most of their branches will change US$ TCs. Banks in larger towns and tourist centres have ATMs. Cash or traveller's cheques (TCs) can be changed in most tourist centres at a competitive rate. Credit cards are widely accepted.

Tipping is commonplace in Indonesia, and small bills are often handed over at the end of every transaction to smooth it over and ensure good service, Indeed, it can often seem that the whole country is founded on tipping, an informal way of channelling money through society so that lower earners can supplement their meagre earnings and are motivated into action. A 10% service charge is added to bills at more expensive hotels. Porters expect to be tipped about 2000Rp a bag. In more expensive restaurants, where no service is charged, a tip of 5-10% may be appropriate. Taxi drivers (in larger towns) appreciate a small tip (1000Rp). *Parkirs* always expect payment for 'watching' your vehicle; 1000Rp.

Cost of travelling

Indonesia is no longer the bargain country it was 10 years ago. Whilst it is still cheap by Western standards tourists can now expect to dig deeper for their meals and accommodation. Visitors staying in 1st-class hotels and eating in top-notch restaurants will probably spend between US100 and US$150 a day. Tourists on a mid-range budget, staying in cheaper a/c accommodation and eating in local restaurants, will probably spend between US$50-80 a day. A backpacker, staying in fan-cooled guesthouses and eating cheaply, could scrape by on US$20-25 a day, though this leaves little room for wild partying. Indonesia has seen prices spiral in recent years, particularly for food and this is reflected in the increased costs that travellers now have to bear when visiting the country.

Post

The postal service is relatively reliable; though important mail should be registered. Every town and tourist centre has either a *kantor pos* (post office) or postal agent, where you can buy stamps, post letters and parcels.

Safety

Despite the recent media coverage of terrorist plots and attacks, riots and other disturbances in Indonesia, it remains a safe country and violence against foreigners is rare. Petty theft is a minor problem.

Avoid carrying large amounts of cash; TCs can be changed in most major towns.

Beware of the confidence tricksters who are widespread in tourist areas. Sudden reports of unbeatable bargains or closing down sales are usual ploys.

Civil unrest The following areas of Indonesia have seen disturbances in recent years and visits are not recommended: Maluku (around Ambon), Central Sulawesi (around Palu and Poso). Both these places have been victims of sectarian violence.

However, these incidents have been localized and almost never affected foreign visitors. Embassies ask visitors to exercise caution when travelling in Aceh, a region recovering from a long internal conflict.

Flying   After a series of accidents the EU banned many Indonesian airlines from entering its air space over continuing concerns of poor maintenance and safety. The Indonesian government and airline companies have taken this very seriously and the last few years have seen brand new Boeings and Airbuses being rolled out by **Lion Air** and **Garuda**. The airlines considered acceptable by the EU are **Batavia**, **Garuda** and **Indonesia AirAsia.** Many European embassies advise against domestic air travel. For the latest information, see www.fco.gov.uk/en and www.travel.state.gov/travel/warnings.html.

Telephone → *Country code +62.*
Operator T101. International enquiries T102. Local enquiries T108. Long-distance enquiries T106. Every town has its communication centres (**Wartel**), where you can make local and international calls and faxes.

Mobile phones   Known as hand-phones or HP in Indonesia, use has sky rocketed and costs are unbelievably low. It usually costs around 15,000Rp to by a Sim card with a number. Top-up cards are sold at various denominations. If you buy a 10,000Rp or 20,000Rp card, the vendor will charge a few more thousand, in order to gain some profit. If you buy a 100,000Rp card, you will pay a few thousand less than 100,000Rp. This is standard practice throughout the country. Beware of vendors in Kuta, Bali who try and sell Sim cards at highly inflated prices. Reliable operators include **Telkomsel**, **IM3** and **Pro XL**. If you want to buy a dirt cheap phone in country, look for the Esia brand which offers bargain basement phone and credit packages.

Tax
Expect to pay 11% tax in the more expensive restaurants, particularly in tourist areas of Bali and Lombok. Some cheaper restaurants serving foreigners may add 10% to the bill.

Airport tax   75,000Rp-150,000Rp on international flights (Jakarta and Denpasar are both 150,000Rp), and anywhere between 10,000Rp and 30,000Rp on domestic flights, depending on the airport.

Visas and immigration
Visitors from several nations, including Malaysia, The Philippines and Singapore are allowed a visa-free stay of 30 days in Indonesia. Visitors from nations including the following are able to get a US$25 30-day **Visa On Arrival** (**VOA**): Australia, Canada, France, Germany, Holland, Ireland, Italy, New Zealand, Portugal, Spain, United Kingdom and the USA. Check with your embassy. Pay at a booth at the port of entry. These visas are extendable at immigration offices in the country for an extra 30 days. In Bali many travel agents offer to extend visas, for a fee.Visitors wishing to obtain a VOA must enter and leave Indonesia though certain ports of entry, including the following:

Sea ports   Batam, Tanjung Uban, Belawan (Medan), Dumai, Jayapura, Tanjung Balaikarimun, Bintang Pura (Tanjung Pinang), and Kupang.

Airports   Medan, Pekanbaru, Padang, Jakarta, Surabaya, Bali, Manado, Adisucipto in Yogyakarta, Adisumarmo in Solo, and Selaparang in Mataram, Lombok.

A US$10 VOA (7 days) is available for visitors to the Riau islands of Batam and Bintan.

60-day visitor visas (B211) are available at Indonesian embassies and consulates around the world (a ticket out of the country, 2 photos and a completed visa form is necessary). Costs vary. They can be extended giving a total stay of 6 months (must be extended at an immigration office in Indonesia each month after the initial 60-day visa has expired; take it to the office 4 days before expiry). To extend the visa in Indonesia, a fee of US$25 is levied and a sponsor letter from a local person is needed. To obtain a 60-day visitor visa in Singapore, a one-way ticket from Batam to Singapore is adequate: purchase from the ferry centre at HarbourFront in Singapore.

It is crucial to check this information before travelling as the visa situation in Indonesia is extremely volatile. Travellers who overstay their visa will be fined US$20 a day. Long-term overstayers can expect a fine and jail sentence. See www.indonesianembassy. org.uk for more information.

All visitors to Indonesia must possess a passport valid for at least 6 months from their date of arrival in Indonesia, and they should have proof of onward travel. It is not uncommon for immigration officers to ask to see a ticket out of the country. (A Batam–Singapore ferry ticket or cheap Medan–Penang air ticket will suffice).

Contents

Jakarta

Jakarta is Indonesia's centre of commerce and communications, of manufacturing activity and consumption, of research and publishing. It has the highest per capita income and the greatest concentration of rupiah billionaires. Jakarta is not often rated very highly as a tourist attraction, but if visitors can tolerate the traffic, then it is possible to spend an enjoyable few days visiting the excellent museums, admiring the architectural heritage of the Dutch era, strolling through the old harbour or discovering some of the many antique, arts and crafts shops. Night owls are invariably bowled over by the city's nightlife, which offers superb variety, from sipping top-notch vintages in lounge bars to downright dirty clubbing.

Today, Jakarta is a sprawling, cosmopolitan city, with a population of over 9,580,000 (2010 census)– making it by far the largest city in Indonesia. Metropolitan Jakarta, known as Jabodetabek (metropolitan Jakarta includes the satellite cities of Bogor, Depok, Tangerang and Bekasi), has an estimated population of 28 million, making it one of the 10 largest metropolitan areas on earth. Growth has been rapid. Jakarta is perceived by the poorer rural Indonesians as a city paved with gold, and they have flocked to the capital in their thousands.

The central area is dominated by office blocks, international hotels, flashy condominium developments, shopping malls and wide, tree-lined roads. Off the main thoroughfares, the streets become smaller and more intimate, almost village-like. These are the densely inhabited kampungs where immigrants have tended to live – one-storey, tile-roofed houses crammed together and linked by a maze of narrow paths. Initially, kampungs developed their own identity, with people from particular language and ethnic groups, even from particular towns, congregating in the same place and maintaining their individual identities. Today those distinctions are less obvious, but the names of the kampungs are a reminder of their origins: Kampung Bali, Kampung Aceh (North Sumatra) and Kampung Makassar (Ujung Pandang), for example.

Ins and outs → *Phone code: 021.*

Tourist information
The **Jakarta Tourist Office** ⓘ *Jakarta Theatre Building, Jln MH Thamrin 9, T021 314 2067, Mon-Sat 0900-1800, www.jakarta-tourism. go.id*, supplies maps and information.

Sights → *For listings see pages 30-40.*

Kota or Old Batavia
ⓘ *From the Hotel Indonesia roundabout or the Sarinah building take TransJakarta bus corridor 1 to Jakarta Kota Station or a taxi.*

The city of Jakarta developed from the small area known as **Kota**, which stretches from the Pasar Ikan (Fish Market) to Jalan Jembatan Batu, just south of Kota train station. The area is about 8 km north of both Monas and many of the city's hotels and guesthouses. North of Pasar Ikan was the old harbour town of **Sunda Kelapa** ⓘ *admission to harbour area 1500Rp, daily 0800-1800*, which thrived from the 12th century to 1527 and is still worth a visit today. *Sunda* refers to the region of West Java and *Kelapa* means coconut. Impressive Bugis or Makassar schooners dock here on their inter-island voyages and can be seen moored along the wharf. Gradually, they are being supplanted by modern freighters, but for the time being at least it is possible to see these graceful ships being loaded and unloaded by wiry barefoot men, who cross precariously between the wharf and the boats along narrow planks. Boatmen will offer visitors the chance to ride in a small boat around the harbour, which gives a fascinating glimpse into life on the water. A 30-minute trip should cost between 40,000Rp and 50,000Rp, but hard bargaining is required. It is also sometimes possible to arrange a passage on one of the boats to Kalimantan and elsewhere.

On the southern edge of Sunda Kelapa and close to the Lookout Tower (see below) is the original, and still functioning, **Pasar Ikan**. The market is an odd mixture of ship

1 Jakarta

➜ Jakarta maps
1 Jakarta, page 23
2 Kota, page 24
3 Jakarta centre, page 27

Sleeping ▣
Kamar Kamar 1

Eating ❼
Anatolia 1
Apartment 2
Gourmet Garage 3
Kinara 4
Loewy 5
Trattoria 6

Bars & clubs ❶
CJs 8
Elbow Room 7
Red Square 11
Stadium 12
Vin + 13
Vino Embassy 14

chandlers, tourist stalls and food outlets. Among the merchandise on sale are sea shells, toy *kijangs*, carvings and unfortunate stuffed animals. Close by at Jalan Pasar Ikan 1 is the **Bahari (Maritime) Museum** ① *T021 669 3406, Tue-Sun 0900-1500, 2000Rp,* which was one of the original Dutch warehouses used for storing spices, coffee and tea. Today it is home to an unimpressive maritime collection. However, upstairs is an interesting display of photographs dating from the late 19th and early 20th centuries, recording life on board the steamships that linked Batavia with Holland. The museum is worth a visit for the building rather than its contents. Other warehouses behind this museum were built between 1663 and 1669.

Overlooking the fetid **Kali Besar (Big Canal)**, choked with rubbish and biologically dead, is the **Uitkijk (Lookout Tower)** ① *daily 0900-1700, 2000Rp,* built in 1839 on the walls of the Dutch fortress Bastion Culemborg (itself constructed in 1645). The tower was initially used to spy on (and signal to) incoming ships, and later as a meteorological post – a role it continued to fill until this century. From the top of the tower there are views north over the port of Sunda Kelapa and south to the city, over an area of poor housing and urban desolation.

2 **Kota**

➜ Jakarta maps
1 Jakarta, page 23
2 Kota, page 24
3 Jakarta centre, page 27

200 metres
200 yards

Sleeping ▦
Batavia 1

Eating ●
Café Batavia 1

Less than 1 km from the Bahari Museum and Sunda Kelapa, south along either Jalan Cangkeh or Jalan Kapak, is one of the last **Dutch-era drawbridges** across the Kali Besar. It was built over two centuries ago and is known as the 'Chicken Market Bridge', but it has been allowed to fall into disrepair. Continuing south for another 200 m or so, walking past old Dutch warehouses, godowns and other commercial buildings, is **Fatahillah Square**, or **Taman Fatahillah**. This was the heart of the old Dutch city and the site of public executions and punishments – hangings, death by impalement and public floggings. It was also a bustling market place. In the middle of the square is a small, domed building (rebuilt in 1972), the site of the old drinking fountain. The Dutch were unaware that the water from this fountain was infested and it contributed to the city's high incidence of cholera and consequently high mortality rate. On the south side of the square is the **Fatahillah Museum**, on the site of the first City Hall built in 1620. A second hall was constructed in 1627 and today's building was completed in 1710. A fine example of Dutch architecture (reminiscent of the old city hall of Amsterdam), it became a military headquarters after independence and finally, in 1974, the **Museum of the History of Jakarta** ⓘ *T021 692 9101, Tue-Sun 0900-1500, 2000Rp.* It is a lovely building but, like so many Indonesian museums, the collection is poorly laid out. It contains Dutch furniture and VOC memorabilia. In the courtyard behind the museum, two *ondel-ondel* figures stand outside another room of rather down-at-heel exhibits. Below the main building are the prison cells.

The **Wayang Museum** ⓘ *on the west side of the square at Jln Pintu Besar Utara 27, T021 682 9560, Tue-Sun 0900-1500, 2000Rp,* was previously called the Museum of Old Batavia. All that remains of the original 1912 building is its facade. Until 1974 it housed the collection now in the Fatahillah Museum and today contains a good collection of *wayang kulit* and *wayang golek* puppets. Well-made examples are sold here for US$22-77. Performances of *wayang kulit* or *wayang golek* are occasionally held here (enquire at tourist office). West from the Wayang Museum and over the Kali Besar (canal) is the **Toko Merah** or **Red House**. This was once the home of Governor-General Gustaaf van Imhoff. There are some other interesting 18th-century Dutch buildings in the vicinity.

On the north side of Fatahillah Square is an old Portuguese bronze cannon called **Si Jagur**, brought to Batavia by the Dutch after the fall of Melaka in 1641. The design of a clenched fist is supposed to be a symbol of cohabitation and it is visited by childless women in the hope that they will be rendered fertile. On the east side of the square is the **Balai Seni Rupa** (**Fine Arts Museum**), formerly the Palace of Justice at Jalan Pos Kota 2. Built in the 1860s, it houses a poor exhibition of paintings by Indonesian artists. The building is shared with the **Museum Keramik** ⓘ *T021 690 7062, Tue-Sun 0900-1500, 2000Rp,* a collection of badly displayed ceramics. The most stylish place to eat and drink on the square is at the **Café Batavia** – itself something of an architectural gem in Indonesian terms. It was built in stages between 1805 and 1850 and is the second oldest building on the square (after the City Hall). Particularly fine is the renovated Grand Salon upstairs, made of Java teak. The café was opened at the end of 1993 and is frequented by foreigners and the Indonesian wealthy. There is a **tourist information office** next to the café and, next to this, a **clothes market,** which functions every day except Sunday.

East of Kota railway station on the corner of Jalan Jembatan Batu and Jalan Pangeran is the oldest church in Jakarta, **Gereja Sion** ⓘ *admission by donation in the adjacent church office,* also known as the 'old Portuguese Church' or 'Gereja Portugis'. It was built for the so-called 'Black Portuguese' – Eurasian slaves brought to Batavia by the Dutch from Portuguese settlements in India and Ceylon. These slaves were promised freedom, provided that they converted to the Dutch Reformed Church. The freed men and women became a social group known as *Mardijkers* (Liberated Ones). The church was built in 1693 and is a fine example of the Baroque style, with a handsome carved wooden pulpit and an elaborately carved organ. The four chandeliers are of yellow copper.

Central Jakarta

South of Fatahillah Square is **Glodok**, or **Chinatown**. This lies outside the original city walls and was the area where the Chinese settled after the massacre of 1740. Despite a national ban on the public display of Chinese characters that was only rescinded in August 1994, Glodok's warren of back streets still feels like a Chinatown, with shophouses, enterprise and activity, and temples tucked behind shop fronts. Midway between Fatahillah Square and Merdeka Square is the **National Archives** or **Arsip Nasional**. This building (which no longer holds the National Archives) was erected in 1760 as a country house for Reiner de Klerk, a wealthy resident who subsequently became governor-general. Since 1925, it has been owned by the state and now houses an interesting collection of Dutch furniture.

The enormous **Medan Merdeka (Liberty Square)** dominates the centre of Jakarta. It measures 1sq km and is one of the largest city squares in the world. In the centre of Medan Merdeka is the **National Monument (Monas)**, a 137-m-high pinnacle meant to represent a *lingga* and thus symbolize fertility and national independence. This massive obelisk was commissioned by President Sukarno in 1961 to celebrate Indonesia's independence from the Dutch. Construction entailed the bulldozing of a large squatter community to make way for the former president's monumental ambitions. It is known among residents of the city, rather irreverently, as Sukarno's Last Erection. Covered in Italian marble, it is topped by a bronze flame (representing the spirit of the revolutionaries), coated in 35 kg of gold leaf. Take the lift to the observation platform for magnificent views over the city. In the basement below the monument is a **museum** ① *T021 384 2777, daily 0830-1700 (closed last Mon of the month), 7500Rp for the museum and trip to the top of the structure; for 2750Rp visitors can access the museum and the lower part of the structure, ticket booth to the north of the monument; avoid going at weekends when there are long queues and general mayhem, as tourists from all over the country descend on the site for a visit.* This houses dioramas depicting the history of Indonesia's independence. The entrance to the museum is north of the road immediately in front of the monument (access is through an underground tunnel), where there is a **statue of Diponegoro** (a Javanese hero) on horseback. He was held prisoner by the Dutch at the Batavia town hall, before being exiled to Manado in North Sulawesi.

On the west side of the square is the neoclassical **National Museum** ① *T021 386 8172, Sun, Tue-Thu 0830-1430, Fri 0830-1130, Sat 0830-1330, 750Rp, guided English-language tours available at 1030 on Tue and Thu, see the Jakarta Post for details as times and days vary, or call the Indonesian Heritage Society on T021 572 5870.* Established in 1860 by the Batavian Fine Arts Society, it is an excellent museum and well worth a visit. Set around a courtyard, the collection consists of some fine stone sculpture (mostly of Hindu gods), a textile collection, and a collection of mainly Chinese ceramics found in Indonesia. Next to the ceramics is a display of bronzeware, including some magnificent Dongson drums and krisses. The pre-history room is well laid out. Its collection includes the skull cap and thigh bone of Java Man, a rare example of *Homo erectus*. The ethnographic collection includes an excellent range of masks, puppets, household articles, musical instruments and some models of traditional buildings representing cultures from several of the main islands in the archipelago. There is also a handicraft shop.

On the north side of the square is the neoclassical **Presidential Palace** or **Istana Merdeka**, built in 1861 and set in immaculate gardens. Originally named **Koningsplein Paleis**. President Sukarno resided at the Istana Merdeka, but President Suharto moved to a more modest residence and the building is now only used for state occasions. Behind the palace is the older **State Palace (Istana Negara)**, next to the Bina Graha (the presidential office building). This palace was built for a Dutchman at the end of the 18th century and was the official residence of Dutch governors-general, before the Koningsplein Palace was built. To get to the State Palace, walk down Jalan Veteran 3 and turn west on Jalan Veteran.

In the northeast corner of Medan Merdeka is the impressive **Istiqlal Mosque**, finished in 1978 after more than 10 years' work. The interior is simple and is almost entirely constructed of marble. It is the principal place of worship for Jakarta's Muslims and reputedly the largest mosque in Southeast Asia, with room for more than 10,000 worshippers. Non-Muslims can visit the mosque when prayers are not in progress. Facing the mosque, in the northwest corner of Lapangan Banteng, is the strange neo-Gothic **Catholic Cathedral**; its date of construction is unknown, but it was restored in 1901.

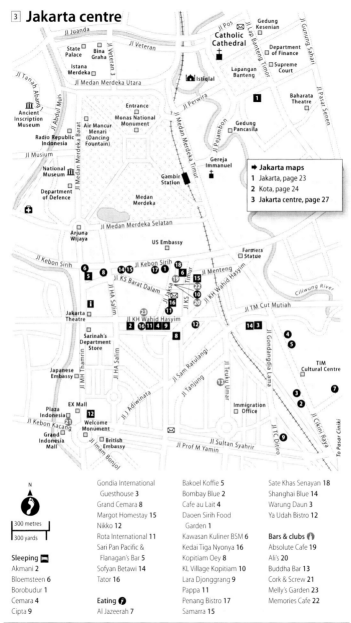

➡ Jakarta maps
1 Jakarta, page 23
2 Kota, page 24
3 Jakarta centre, page 27

N

300 metres
300 yards

Sleeping 🛏
Akmani **2**
Bloemsteen **6**
Borobudur **1**
Cemara **4**
Cipta **9**

Gondia International
 Guesthouse **3**
Grand Cemara **8**
Margot Homestay **15**
Nikko **12**
Rota International **11**
Sari Pan Pacific &
 Flanagan's Bar **5**
Sofyan Betawi **14**
Tator **16**

Eating 🍴
Al Jazeerah **7**

Bakoel Koffie **5**
Bombay Blue **2**
Cafe au Lait **4**
Daoen Sirih Food
 Garden **1**
Kawasan Kuliner BSM **6**
Kedai Tiga Nyonya **16**
Kopitiam Oey **8**
KL Village Kopitiam **10**
Lara Djonggrang **9**
Pappa **11**
Penang Bistro **17**
Samarra **15**

Sate Khas Senayan **18**
Shanghai Blue **14**
Warung Daun **3**
Ya Udah Bistro **12**

Bars & clubs 🍸
Absolute Cafe **19**
Ali's **20**
Buddha Bar **13**
Cork & Screw **21**
Melly's Garden **23**
Memories Cafe **22**

From the south corner of Lapangan Banteng, Jalan Pejambon runs south past **Gedung Pancasila**, the building where Sukarno gave his famous *proklamasi*, outlining the five principles of Pancasila. At the southern end of Jalan Pejambon, backing onto Merdeka Square, is the **Gereja Immanuel**, an attractive circular domed church built by Dutch Protestants in the classical style in 1835.

West of the city centre

The **Textile Museum** ① *Jln Satsuit Tuban 4, near the Tanah Abang Market (and railway station), T021 560 6613, Tue-Sun 0900-1500, 2000Rp*, is housed in an airy Dutch colonial house set back from the road. It contains a good range of Indonesian textiles, both batik and *ikat*.

South of the city centre

The **Adam Malik Museum** ① *29 Jln Diponegoro, west from the junction with Jln Surabaya, Tue-Sat 1000-1300, Sun 0930-1300, 2500Rp, get there by bus or taxi*, houses a private, quirky collection that includes cameras, radios, walking sticks and watches, as well as Chinese ceramics, woodcarving from Papua, stone carvings from Java, ostentatious furniture, guns, krisses and some interesting Russian icons. The problem with this museum is its lack of discrimination. The interesting and the commonplace, the skilled and the inept, are all massed together.

A night-time drive, or perhaps even a walk, down **Jalan Latuharhary** in Menteng, reveals a seedier – or at least an alternative – side of life in Jakarta. Transvestites, dressed up to the nines, and known as *banci* (meaning hermaphrodite or homosexual) or *waria*, hawk their wares. Foreign visitors may be astonished not only by their beauty, but also by the fact that this is countenanced in an otherwise relatively strict Muslim society. Transvestites have, in fact, a long and honourable tradition not just in Indonesia but throughout Southeast Asia.

The large, wholesale **Pasar Cikini**, in the district of Menteng, is worth a visit to see the range of fruit, vegetables, fish and other fresh products trucked in from the surrounding countryside and the coast for sale in Jakarta. The second floor houses a gold market.

Around Jakarta

Taman Mini-Indonesia

① *T021 840 9214, www.tamanmini.com, park admission 9000Rp plus additional charges for major attractions, daily 0800-1700, 18 km and a rather arduous journey by public transport from the city centre – take a TransJakarta bus corridor 7 from Kampung Melayu to Kampung Rambutan terminal and from there an angkot to the park (1-1½ hrs), or a taxi from town for about US$18.*

This is a 120-ha 'cultural park', 10 km southeast of Jakarta (but closer to 20 km from the centre). Completed in 1975, there are 27 houses, each representing one of Indonesia's provinces and built in the traditional style of that region, although the building materials used are modern substitutes. Frustratingly, no translation of the descriptions is offered. All the houses are set around a lake with boats for hire. It is possible to drive around the park on weekdays or, alternatively, walk, take the mini train, cable car or horse and cart (small charges for these). The cable car takes passengers over the lake, upon which there is a replica of the whole archipelago. The **Keong Mas Theatre** ① *daily 1100-1700, from 30,000Rp,* (so-called because its shape resembles a golden snail) presents superb not-to-be-missed films on Indonesia, projected on an enormous IMAX screen. Check *Jakarta Post* for details of screenings. The **Museum Indonesia** ① *0900-1500, 5000Rp,* a Balinese-style building, houses a good collection of arts and crafts and costumes from across the archipelago. The **Museum Komodo** ① *0800-1500, 10,000Rp*, is, as the name suggests, built in the form of the *Varanus komodiensis*, better known as the Komodo dragon. It houses dioramas of Indonesian fauna and flora. There's also an aquarium, an insectarium, an orchid garden, aviaries and a swimming pool.

Pulau Seribu → *For listings, see pages 30-40.*

Pulau Seribu, or 'Thousand Islands', clearly named by the mathematically challenged, actually consists of 112 small islands. Just to the west of Jakarta, off Java's north coast, they are becoming increasingly popular as a tourist destination. The Dutch VOC had a presence on the islands from the 17th century, building forts, churches and shipyards.

Pulau Onrust is one of the closest islands to the mainland. It was used by the Dutch from the early 17th century and became an important ship repair centre; by 1775 as many as 2000 people were living on the island. But in the 1800s the British sacked and burnt the small settlement, so that today only ruins remain. **Pulau Bidadari** also has ruins of a fort and leper hospital built by the VOC. It lies 15 km from Ancol (45 minutes by speedboat). **Pulau Laki** is one of the inner islands situated 3 km offshore from Tanjung Kait west of Jakarta.

Venturing further north into the Java Sea, there are a succession of privately owned resorts including **Pulau Ayer**, **Pulau Putri**, **Pulau Pelangi**, **Pulau Kotok** and **Pulau Panjang**, in that order. They have beautiful beaches and offer snorkelling, scuba-diving, jet skiing and windsurfing.

Krakatau → *For listings, see pages 30-40.*

Krakatau is the site of the largest volcanic eruption ever recorded. The explosion occurred on the morning of the 27 August 1883, had a force equivalent to 2000 Hiroshima bombs, and resulted in the death of 36,000 people. A tsunami 40 m high, radiating outwards at speeds of reportedly over 500 kph, destroyed coastal towns and villages. The explosion was heard from Sri Lanka to Perth in Australia and the resulting waves led to a noticeable surge in the English Channel. The explosion was such that the 400-m-high cone was replaced by a marine trench 300 m deep.

Rupert Furneau writes in his book *Krakatoa* (1965): "At 10 o'clock plus two minutes, three-quarters of Krakatau Island, 11 square miles of its surface, an area not much less than Manhattan, a mass of rock and earth one and one-eighth cubic miles in extent, collapsed into a chasm beneath. Nineteen hours of continuous eruption had drained the magma from the chamber faster than it could be replenished from below. Their support removed, thousands of tons of roof rock crashed into the void below. Krakatau's three cones caved in. The sea bed reared and opened in upheaval. The sea rushed into the gaping hole. From the raging cauldron of seething rocks, frothing magma and hissing sea, spewed an immense quantity of water ... From the volcano roared a mighty blast, Krakatau's death cry, the greatest volume of sound recorded in human history".

In 1927, further volcanic activity caused a new island to rise above the sea – **Anak Krakatau** (Child of Krakatau). Today this island stands 200 m above sea level and visitors may walk from the east side of the island upon the warm, devastated landscape through deep as, to the main crater. It remains desolate and uninhabited, though the other surrounding islands have been extensively recolonized (a process carefully recorded by naturalists; the first visitor after the 1883 explosion noted a spider vainly spinning a web).

Check that the volcano is safe to visit and take thick-soled walking shoes (Krakatau is still avowedly active: between 1927 and 1992 it erupted no less than 73 times). There is good snorkelling and diving in the water around the cliffs; the undersea thermal springs allow abundant marine plant growth and this attracts a wealth of sea creatures, big and small.

The sea crossing is calmest and the weather best from April to June and September to October. Between November and March there are strong currents and often rough seas.

Note Anak Krakatau is currently highly active and tourists are NOT permitted to climb the crater. This is due to spewing molten rocks and potentially fatal toxic gases. Tourists can land on Anak Krakatau for a wander, at their own risk. Check the latest information before heading out, as the volcano has been put on the highest alert several times in the past year.

Jakarta listings

For Sleeping and Eating price codes and other relevant information, see pages 9-11.

🛏 Sleeping

Jakarta *p23, maps p23, p24 and p27*
Jalan Jaksa and around
This small street has been the backpackers' headquarters for years, with a large selection of budget lodgings, cheap eateries and plenty of travel agents. Don't come here expecting Thailand's Khaosan Rd or the tourist quarter of Ho Chi Minh; this street is decidedly low key. Slightly more salubrious hotels are located in the streets around Jln Jaksa.

$$$ The Akmani, Jln Wahid Hasyim 91, T021 3190 5335, www.akmanihotel.com. Slick hotel with excellent promo rates and a good range of facilities including pool and bar with pleasant outdoor seating, gym, restaurant and Wi-Fi access (chargeable). The rooms are modern and sleek and the more expensive rooms on the higher floors offer excellent city views. Recommended.

$$$ Cemara Hotel, Jln Wahid Hasyim 69, T021 314 7580, www.hotelcemara.com. Newish place with 60 modern rooms with flatscreen cable TV and bathrooms with tub. Good discounts available. Breakfast not included. Wi-Fi available (chargeable).

$$$-$$ Cipta Hotel, Jln Wahid Hasyim 53, T021 390 4701, www.ciptahotel.com. Excellent service, although the mint

walls and green carpet in some rooms are nauseating. Rooms are clean and spacious with cable TV and fridge. Wi-Fi is available for free in the café downstairs for 10,000Rp per hr. Tax and breakfast included in the price.

$$$-$$ Grand Cemara, Jln Cemara 1, T021 390 8215, www.hotelcemara.com. For those who have travelled halfway around the world to get to Indonesia, this hotel is a fairly comfy mid-range spot to get over the jetlag. Rooms are clean, and come with fridge and cable TV, and some have baths. Expensive internet available in the room. Spa service available. Breakfast not included in the price.

$$ Hotel Tator, Jln Jaksa 37, T021 3192 3940. Selection of a/c and fan rooms, which are a little faded but compare better than most of the other cheap Jaksa options.

$$ Margot Homestay, Jln Jaksa 15C, T021 391 3830. Well-run place with a selection of a/c rooms with TV and decrepit furniture. There's a fair restaurant by the reception.

$$ Rota International Hotel, Jln Wahid Hasyim 63, T021 315 2858. Plenty of choice, with a selection of clean a/c rooms (some are a bit dark, ask to see a selection) with TV and bath around a massive central courtyard.

$ Bloemsteen Hostel, Jln Kebon Sirih Timur 1, 175 (just off Jln Jaksa), T021 3192 3002. This has been the budget traveller's most popular choice for years now, and justifiably remains in pole position with small, spotless rooms and clean shared bathrooms. There is a pleasant balcony upstairs. It's often very busy, so booking ahead is wise.

Menteng and Cikini
There's a range of mid-priced accommodation scattered throughout this area.

$$$-$$ Hotel Sofyan Betawi, Jln Cut Meutia 9, T021 314 0695, www.sofyan hotel.com. Popular with Indonesian business people. Has clean, comfortable rooms (some are a bit dark), with TV and bath. Broadband access.

$ Gondia International Guesthouse, Jln Gondangdia Kecil 22, T021 390 9221. Set down a small alley off Jln Gondangdia, this friendly place has decent, simple a/c rooms with TV and a small but pleasant garden.

Soekarno-Hatta Airport
$$$ Jakarta Airport Hotel, Terminal 2 (above Arrivals area), T021 559 0008, www.jakartaairporthotel.com. Super location in airport for those with a layover, or arriving late at night. Rooms are smart and have a/c and cable TV. There is also a half-day (maximum 6 hrs stay) rate of US$75.

Elsewhere
$$$$-$$ Hotel Borobudur, Jln Lapangan Banteng Selatan, T021 380 5555, www.hotelborobudur.com. This old dame is aging well, with friendly rather than stuffy service and a huge selection of rooms. The 693 rooms are set in rambling corridors reminiscent of *The Shining*, seemingly endless. Standard rooms are comfy, although a little aged. There is a raised seating area by the window with views over the hotel's extensive grounds.

$$$$-$$$ Hotel Nikko, Jln MH Thamrin 59, T021 230 1122, www.nikkojakarta.com. Japanese minimalist style is in evidence aplenty here in the gorgeous design. Rooms are clean, modern with top fabrics and plenty of space. Facilities include pool, fitness centre and restaurants, some with amazing views of the skyline. There is a shuttle bus from here to Plaza Indonesia (no more than 5 mins' walk), which gives some idea of the clientele.

$$$$-$$$ Sari Pan Pacific, Jln MH Thamrin, T021 390 2707, www.panpacific.com/jakarta. Busy business hotel, with intriguing facade. The carpeted a/c rooms are well decorated, although the beds look ancient, and have cable TV, bath and broadband access. Facilities include pool and fitness centre. Breakfast for 1 included in the price.

$$$ The Batavia Hotel (formerly Omni Batavia), Jln Kali Besar Barat 44-46, T021 690 4118, www.batavia-hotel.com. Stuck out on a limb down in Kota, this 4-star place is handy for a quick sightseeing trip around the old city, but not much else, and getting a cab from here takes some time. However, the price is not bad considering the good service, and clean rooms with cable TV and big, comfy beds. Pool, fitness centre.

$$ Kamar Kamar, Jln RS Fatmawati 37K, T021 751 2560, www.kamar-kamar.com. New backpacker hostel with a variety of rooms, though mostly dorms, to the south of the city centre. Very comfortable and with a good rooftop café with occasional live music. Free Wi-Fi throughout. Recommended.

ⓔ Eating

Jakarta *p23, maps p23, p24 and p27*
Jakarta is the best place in Indonesia to eat, with a diverse collection of restaurants spread out all over the city and a growing middle class willing to dip ever deeper into their pockets to fulfil gourmet fantasies.

Go to www.sendokgarpu.com to check what's currently hot in the Jakarta dining and nightlife scene.

Jalan Jaksa and around

$$$-$$ Samarra, Jln Kebon Sirih 77, T021 391 8690. Open 1100-2300. Gorgeous Arabic decor lends a sense of opulence to this restaurant serving Arab-Indonesian fusion food. The speciality of the house is *sate* served with numerous delectable sauces. There is an excellent wine list and sheesha pipes are available. Belly dancers on Fri and Sat evenings. Recommended.

$$$-$$ Shanghai Blue, Jln Kebon Sirih 79, T021 391 8690. Open 1100-2300. Owned by the same group that runs **Samarra** next door, the decor here is similarly beautiful with modern, funky Chinese seating, 1920s portraits of Shanghainese ladies adorning the walls and sultry lighting. The fare is Betawi (local Jakarta)-Chinese fusion, with some interesting spins on the local cuisine. Marci, a renowned local singer, charms audiences on Wed and Fri nights.

$$ Kedai Tiga Nyonya, Jln Wahid Hasyim 73, T021 830 8360. Open 1100-2200. Peranakan (Straits Chinese) cuisine in a homely setting. This is a good place to try some *asam pedas* (hot and sour) dishes, or *soka* (soft crab).

$$ Kopitiam Oey, Jln Agus Salim 18. Open 0700-2300. Located in a freshly painted pink shophouse, this is a café offers a fantastic range of Indonesian breakfast dishes and light meals throughout the day. Those in the mood for something heavy will want to dig in to the biryanis on offer.

$$ Penang Bistro, Jln Kebon Sirih 59, T021 319 0600. Open 1100-2200. Malaysian favourites served in sleek, clean a/c setting. Dishes include Hainan chicken rice, *roti canai* (Indian bread served with curry) and *kangkung belachan* (water spinach with prawn-based chilli sauce).

$$ Ya Udah Bistro, Jln Johar 15 Gondangia, T021 314 0349. Popular hang-out with a lengthy menu of central European favourites. The Strammer Max, described as a German trucker's breakfast is sure to keep energy levels high for a morning of exploring. Recommended.

$ Daoen Siri Food Garden, Jln Kebon Sirih 41, T021 316 1200. Collection of stalls serving an enticing array of regional Indonesian cuisine inside a rather wobbly looking traditional thatched structure.

$ Kawasan Kuliner BSM, in a lane next to the Sari Pan Pacific connecting Jln Thamrin and Jln Agus Salim. A lane lined with tables and *kaki lima* stalls serving a huge variety of cheap Indonesian fare. Popular with office workers at lunchtime and a fun introduction to Indonesian street fare.

$ KL Village Kopitiam, Jln Jaksa 21-23, T021 314 8761. Open 0700-0100. Outdoor Malaysian eatery that has shaken up the scene on Jaksa with its delicious curries, *nasi lemak* (rice cooked in coconut milk with side dishes), and good-value set meals. Recommended.

$ Pappa Restaurant, Jln Jaksa 41, T021 3192 3452. Open 24 hrs. Cheap Western and Indonesian fare served round the clock to feed the hordes of drunken English teachers who need a burger and just 1 more beer before home.

$ Sate Khas Senayan, Jln Kebon Sirih 31A, T021 3192 6238. Open 1000-2200. This is an excellent place to try *sate*. Set in a spotless clean environment, the restaurant serves up divine portions of chicken and beef *sate* along with good Javanese rice dishes, and some divine icy delights for dessert.

Kemang

Affectionately and somewhat optimistically known as Little Bali, this area is a popular haunt for expats with money to burn on top-class dining. Traffic around here is notoriously nightmarish, and it can take almost 1 hr to get here from central and north Jakarta.

$$$-$$ Anatolia, Jln Kemang Raya 110A, T021 719 4617. Open 1100-2300. Sumptuous Ottoman decor, sheesha pipes and superb Turkish cuisine make this one of the city's most respected restaurants.

$$$-$$ Gourmet Garage, Jln Kemang Raya, T021 719 0875. Open 1000-2300.

Smart collection of stalls including an oyster bar and a Japanese counter. There is a supermarket downstairs selling cheeses, meats, bread and all the things homesick Westerners crave.

$$$-$$ Kinara, Jln Kemang Raya 78B, T021 719 2677. This place does Moghul architecture proud with its wonderful facade and interior. Tasty fare; the tandoori is well worth trying.

Elsewhere

$$$ The Apartment, Menara Gracia, GF, Jln HR Rasuna Said. Open 0830-2400. Homesick meat fans will want to head here for their delectable steak and eggs and wagyu beef cheek. Trades well on its novelty of offering diners a choice of apartment room to dine in including a jacuzzi and a bedroom.

$$$ Lara Djonggrang, Jln Teuku Cik Di Tiro 4, Menteng, T021 315 3252. Superlative Indonesian dining experience and ideal for those with a little cash to splash and some romance in mind. Excellent array of Javanese fare including Javanese baby chicken and *soto daging madura* (beef slices in a coconut broth with candlenut paste and lime). Recommended.

$$$-$$ Al Jazeerah Restaurant, Jln Raden Saleh 58, T021 314 6108. Open 1000-2300. This street is packed full of authentic Arab eateries, and this is one of the best with dishes such as hummous, tabbouleh and plenty of kebabs on offer. No booze.

$$ Bombay Blue, Jln Cikini Raya 40, T021 316 2865. Open 1200-2300. Slick decor and tasty Indian cuisine. Long menu featuring a good range of non-veg and veg dishes.

$$ Café Batavia, Taman Fatahillah, T021 691 5531. Open 0800-0100. Business is no longer as brisk as it once was, but this place still remains a classic venue, for a drink if nothing else. The bar is resonant with times past, with high ceilings, slowly whirring ceiling fans and 1920s class. Fare is Asian and Western.

$$ Loewy, Jln Lingkar Mega Kuningan E42 No 1, T021 2554 2378. Open 1100-0200.

Belgian bistro with an excellent selection of wines and coffees and the city's finest selection of single malt whiskies. Notable dishes include steak, 3-cheese fondue and lamb shank. Recommended.

$$ Trattoria, Menara Karya Building, Jln HR Rasuna Said 1-2, Mega Kuningan, T021 579 4472. Open 0900-2330. Excellent value authentic Italian cuisine, with good house wine and a rather tasty complimentary chocolate liqueur providing the icing on the cake. Recommended.

$$-$ Warung Daun, Jln Cikini Raya 26, T021 391 0909. Open 1100-1000. Popular with Indonesian ladies that lunch, the MSG-free fare, with organic vegetables, is a sure-fire winner. The cuisine is Sundanese and Javanese and features tasty *ikan gurame* (fried carp) and some creative vegetarian dishes.

$ Bakoel Koffie, Jln Cikini Raya 25, T021 3193 6608. Open 1000-2400. Spacious café with pleasant outdoor seating area and newspapers to browse. Plenty of coffees and cakes to indulge in.

$ Café Au Lait, Jln Cikini Raya 17, T021 3983 5094. Open 0800-2400. European-style café, with high ceilings, free Wi-Fi access and a wide range of coffee, cakes, sandwiches and simple pasta dishes. Occasional live music in the evenings.

There are also a large number of foodstalls, such as on **Jln HA Salim**, which has a great number of cheap regional restaurants; **Jln Mangga Besar**, with night-time *warungs*; **Grand Indonesia mall**, which has an excellent foodcourt in the basement and **Pasar Raya**, Blok M, with a variety of reliably good 'stalls' (not just Indonesian) in the basement. The top floor of **Sogo**, in the Plaza Indonesia, has similar stalls; and **Café Tenda Semanggi**, in the middle of the Central Business District, near Bengkel Night Park (taxi drivers know it), is an open-air area that has been used for a cluster of upmarket foodstalls, serving mainly Indonesian cuisine. A really happening place with great atmosphere. People come here more for the vibe than the food. Open 1800-0100.

🎵 Bars and clubs

Jakarta *p23, maps p23, p24 and p27*
If you want to have just 1 massive night out in Indonesia, it has to be in Jakarta, where the sun sets early and the night is long. There is a staggering choice of drinking venues to suit all and sundry. Nightlife is a very friendly affair, and many who go out on the tiles in Jakarta ending up slurping noodles at 0600 with a new group of friends and an impending hangover on the way.

Jalan Jaksa and around
Jln Jaksa has a reputation as being quite downmarket, and the bars conform to that stereotype, with plenty of hookers and local hangers-on. However, an evening out here can be great fun, slightly anarchic and is a great way to meet interesting characters.
Absolute Café, Jln Jaksa 5, T021 3190 9847. Open 1600-0400. A/c bar with pool tables, TVs screening football and cheap drinks popular with the English teaching crowd.
Ali's, Jln Jaksa 25, T021 3190 0807. Open 1000-0300. Known as the African expat's bar of choice, this dark bar has TVs, plenty of nooks, crannies and a small dance floor.
Melly's Garden, IBEC Building, Jln Wahid Hasyim 84-88. Lively student hangout with good music, filthy toilets and decent selection of food and drinks. Good spot to mingle with the young intelligentsia away from the sighty more seedy overtones of Jln Jaksa.
Memories Café, Jln Jaksa 17, T021 316 2548. Open 0900-0300. A Jaksa stalwart, this bar has seen it all. Bar-girls flock here to join other drinkers in antics and occasional karaoke numbers.

Elsewhere
Buddha Bar, Jln Teuku Umar 1, Menteng. Open 1800-0100. This place caused a storm when it first opened with local

Buddhist societies deploring the use of the Buddha's image in a drinking establishment. Nevertheless, after the furore settled down, this plush place has settled into its groove with cool beats and stylish decor
CJs, Hotel Mulia, Jln Afrika Asia Senayan, T021 574 7777. Open 1600-0300. Good live music at this raucous club popular with expats and bar-girls on the prowl.
Cork and Screw, Plaza Indonesia, 1st floor, Jln Thamrin, T021 3199 6659. Open 1100-0200. One of the hottest spots in the city, with over 250 different wines from all over the world. Daily 'Happy Pouring' between 1600 and 1800 offering the chance to sample a selection of featured wines. Excellent wine at good prices, and some fine food. Gets packed at weekends.
Elbow Room, Jln Kemang Raya 24, T021 719 4274. European beer and fondue operation with plenty of friendly vibes, varied menu, live music and one-for-one happy hour on weekdays.
Red Square, Plaza Senayan Arcadia Unit X-210, Jln New Delhi, Pintu 9, T021 5790 1281, www.redsquarejakarta.com. This highly successful lounge bar is currently the place to be seen, with sleek and ultra-modern interior featuring groovy lighting. Vodka-based drinks fly off the shelves.
Stadium, Jln Hayam Wuruk 111, T021 626 3323, www.stadiumjakarta.com. Mon-Thu 2000-0600, Fri-Sun 24 hrs. One of Southeast Asia's most notorious clubs, attracting a loyal crowd of wide-eyed worshippers. This dark venue is a confusing maze, with numerous floors and plenty of sin, echoing with techno beats. There really is nowhere else quite like it. Recommended.
Vin +, Jln Kemang Raya, Jln Kemang Raya 45. Open 1600-0200. Fashionable spot to sip wine and people watch.
Vino Embassy, Jln Kemang Raya 67, T021 719 1333. Open 1600-0200. Swish little bar, with dim lights and massive selection of wine.

🎭 Entertainment

Jakarta *p23, maps p23, p24 and p27*
For a schedule of events, look in the 'Where to Go' section of the *Jakarta Post* and the paper's website. The tourist office should also have an idea of what's going on in the city.

Cinema
The Indonesian way is to provide subtitles rather than to dub, so soundtracks are generally in English. Films usually cost between 20,000Rp and 25,000Rp. Good cinemas can be found in the **Jakarta Theatre Building** (Jln MH Thamrin 9) and at the **Grand Indonesia** mall and **EXMall**.

Cultural shows
Erasmus Huis, Jln HR Rasuna Said S-3, T021 524 1069, www.mfa.nl/erasmushuis/en. Next to the Dutch embassy, cultural events, including interesting lectures, are held here.
Gedung Kesenian, Jln Gedung Kesenian 1, T021 380 8282. This centre organizes *wayang orang* performances, piano recitals, theatre and other cultural events, a modern art gallery is attached to the theatre. Check the website or local media for schedule.
Taman Ismail Marzuki (or **TIM**), just off Jln Cikini Raya, T021 3193 7325, www.tamanismailmarzuki.com. This complex is the focal point of cultural activities in the city with performances almost every night, the centre contains exhibition halls, 2 art galleries, theatres, cinema complex and a planetarium.

🎉 Festivals and events

Jakarta *p23, maps p23, p24 and p27*
Ramadan There is an exodus from Jakarta during this time and services may be reduced. The upside is that there is no traffic.
20 Apr Anniversary of Taman Mini, performances of traditional music and dance.
May Jakarta International Cultural Performance, a festival of music and dance from around Indonesia and also from other areas of Southeast Asia.
22 Jun Anniversary of Jakarta, commemorates the founding of Jakarta. Followed by the Jakarta Fair, www.jakarta fair.biz, which takes place in the PRJ Arena, Kemayoran and lasts for 1 month. Exhibitions, live music and performances, art installations and millions of people milling about.
Aug Jalan Jaksa Street Fair, 7 days of entertainment, including dance and music, Betawi art and plenty of fun and games.
Dec Jakarta International Film Festival, www.jiffest.org, selection of contemporary world and documentary films, as well as Indonesian language and animated pictures. Check local media or website for screenings.

🛍 Shopping

Jakarta *p23, maps p23, p24 and p27*
Fixed-priced stores are becoming more common in Jakarta, but bargaining is still the norm wherever there is no marked price. When buying antiques and handicrafts, bargain down to 30-40% of the original asking price, especially on Jln Surabaya. Shopping malls are a way of life in Jakarta, an escape from the traffic and smog, and new shopping malls are being constructed all the time. Some of the most convenient include **Grand Indonesia**, Jln MH Thamrin 1, with banks, designer clothes stores, bookshops and restaurants (recommended); **Plaza Indonesia**, Jln MH Thamrin Kav 28-30, with top brands, good dining options and beautiful people; **EX Mall**, Jln MH Thamrin Kav 28-30, favouring younger shoppers with high street brands, cinema and fast-food joints; and **Plaza Senayan**, Jln Asia Afrika, 1000-2200. Suave and sophisticated and deliciously cool, with a cinema.

Batik Ardiyanto, Pasar Raya (3rd floor), Jln Iskandarsyah 11/2; **Batik Keris**, Danar Hadi, Jln Raden Saleh 1A; **Batik Semar**, Jln Tomang Raya 54; **Government Batik**

Cooperative (GKBI), Jln Jend Sudirman 28; **Iwan Tirta**, Jln Panarukan 25 or Hotel Borobudur; 1 floor of Pasar Raya (Blok M), is devoted to batik; **Pasar Tanar Abang**, a market west of Merdeka Square, has good modern textiles, batik and *ikat* by the metre; **Srikandi**, Jln Melawai VI/6A.

Bookshops Jakarta is a good place to stock up on reading material, with excellent bookshops such as Kinokuniya in several malls.

Handicrafts Sarinah Department Store has 2 floors of handicrafts and batik from across Indonesia and is located on Jln MH Thamrin (at the intersection with Jln KH Wahid Hasyim). This is a great place to stock up on gifts for home, although if you are heading to other destinations in Java or Bali, it's best to wait, as prices are considerably higher in Jakarta.

Supermarket There is a **Hero** super-market beneath the Sarinah building on Jln MH Thamrin, which sells necessities. Most of the malls have supermarkets.

▲ Activities and tours

Language courses
IALF, Sentra Mulia, Jln Rasuna Said Kav X-6 No 8, T021 521 3350, www.ialf.edu. Offers a variety of Bahasa Indonesia courses.

Tour operators
Most larger hotels have travel agents; this list is not comprehensive. Most will arrange city tours, out-of-town day tours and longer tours throughout Indonesia.

For agents and companies geared to the needs of those on a lower budget, Jln Jaksa is probably the best bet. Bus and train tickets are booked for destinations across the archipelago and other services provided.
Astrindo Tours and Travel, 45-47 Jln Kebon Sirih, T021 230 5151. Professional outfit offering tailor-made tours.

Bayu Buana, Jln Kemang Raya 114, T021 7179 0662, www.bayubuanatravel.com. Branches all over the city, can arrange tickets, tours and help with visas.
Divalina Tour and Travel,
Jln Jaksa 35, T021 314 9330.
Indonesian Heritage Society, T021 572 5870, may be offering city tours. These have been discontinued, but might start up again in the near future. There is a US$22 membership, worthwhile if you want to join several tours or are going to be based in the city.
Krakatau Tours, www.krakatau-tour.com, Office Sunset View Carita, Jln Raya Carita KM10, T0813 8666 88 11. Package tours to Krakatau and Ujong Kulon NP.
Robertur Kencana, Jln Jaksa 20, T021 314 2926. Gets the thumbs up from a lot of travellers.

⊖ Transport

Air
Daily flights to most major cities in Indonesia. Fares are generally good value flying out of Jakarta. **Lion Air** (www.lionair.co.id) and **AirAsia** (www.airasia.com) offer online booking. Those looking for a spectacular flight over the mountains of West Java to Bandung or Panganadaran will want to look into flying in one of **Susi Air**'s Cessna Caravans. These flights depart daily from Halim Airport in east Jakarta. Jakarta to **Pangandaran** flights cost around US$65. Book at **Susi Air Jakarta**, BNI 46 Building 32nd floor, Jln Sudirman Kav I, T021 3929 726.

Bajaj
Bajaj, orange motorized 3-wheelers, Indian made, pronounced *bajai*: sometimes known as 'panzer' bajaj because of their tank-like behaviour. There have been rumours that the government would like to do away with bajajs, as they have been deemed 'anti-humane'. They are already barred from Jakarta's main thoroughfares.

Nonetheless, they remain the cheapest way to get around other than by bus or on foot. Negotiate the price furiously before boarding and expect to pay a minimum of 10,000Rp for a short journey.

Many bajaj now run on CNG (Compressed Natural Gas), similar to ones seen in Delhi, and are significantly greener than the standard (painted red) smoke belching motorized models. The government eventually hopes to replace all motorized bajaj with CNG vehicles in an attempt to help clear some of the city's horrific air pollution. CNG bajaj are painted blue.

Boat

Jakarta's port is **Tanjung Priok**, 15 km from the city centre. Take bus No 60 from Jln Pos or bus No P14 from Jln Kebon Sirih, off Jln Jaksa. Or take a taxi. Allow at least 1 hr. It is less than 1 km from the bus station at Tanjung Priok to the dock. The state-owned shipping company **PELNI** has its head office at Jln Gajah Mada 14, T021 633 4342/45. Its ticket office is at Jln Angkasa 20, T021 421 1921. Check the latest schedule at www.pelni.co.id. A counter on the 2nd floor of the building is much less crowded for ticket purchase (entrance on right of building). 2 photocopies of passport are required (photocopying shop on left of building, as you face it). The PELNI ships *Kelud* (for **North Sumatra**, **Riau**), *Leuser* (**Kalimantan**, **Java**), *Dobonsolo* (**Sulawesi**, **Kalimantan**), B*ukit Raya* (**Kalimantan**, **Riau**) *Ciremai* (**Sulawesi**, **Maluku**, **Papua**), *Lambelo* (**Sulawesi**, **Maluku**, **Riau**), *Sirimau* (**Sulawesi**, **Nusa Tenggara**), and *Bukit Sigantung* (**Nusa Tenggara**, **Maluku**, **Sulawesi**, **Papua**), dock here.

Bus

Local Most fares around town are 2500Rp. Crowded, especially during rush hour, and beware of pickpockets.

The **Jakarta Transjarkarta** bus lines have taken a little away from the stress of city travelling, with clean a/c buses travelling along designated corridors that are for these buses only. There are 10 lines running at the moment, although 5 more are in construction. Fares from point to point are 3500Rp, including any transits.
Corridor 1: Blok M–Jln Jend Sudirman–Jln MH Thamrin–Merderka Barat–Harmoni–Jln Gajah Mada–Stasiun Kota.
Corridor 3: Kalideres (bus terminal)–Daan Mogot–Tomang Raya–Harmoni.
Corridor 7: Kampung Rambutan (bus terminal)–Otto Iskandardinata–Letjend MT Haryono.

Booking bus tickets: private bus companies have their offices at these terminals. Travel agents along Jln Jaksa will help tourists get tickets. Another option is to ring the company and reserve a ticket, and pay for it on arrival at the terminal. Your hotel should be able to help you do this. Make sure you find out which terminal your bus from Jakarta departs from. Companies worth trying include: **Lorena**, Jln Hasyim Ashan 15C, T021 634 1166, and **Pahala Kencana**, Komp. Gading Bukit Indah Blok C No 1, Jl Bukit Gading Raya Kelapa Gading, T021 451 7375.

Long distance There are 4 city bus terminals, all some distance from the city centre. **Kalideres Terminal**, on the west edge of the city, 15 km from the centre, serves the west coast, including **Merak** with a handful of connections on to **Sumatra** (most Sumatra buses depart from the Pulo Gadung terminal). Take Transjakarta busway corridor 3 buses to get here. **Kampung Rambutan**, about 15 km south of the city, serves **Bogor**, **Bandung** and other towns and cities in West Java. Take Transjakarta busway corridor 7 buses to get here. **Pulo Gadung Terminal**, 12 km east of the centre at the junction of Jln Bekasi Timur Raya and Jln Perintis Kemerdekaan, serves Central and East Java including the towns of **Cirebon** (5 hrs), **Yogya** (12 hrs), **Surabaya** (15 hrs) and **Malang** (18 hrs). Pulo Gadung is also the main bus terminal for **Sumatra**, with buses going to all the major towns – even as far as **Banda Aceh**, some 3000 km north. **Bali** is served from Pulo Gadung. Lebakbulus Terminal has buses going to **Bandung** and **Bali**. This terminal is 10 km south of the city.

Fares from Jakarta include: **Denpasar** (24 hrs) US$38, **Surabaya** (18 hrs) US$24, **Probolinggo** (20 hrs) US$26, **Yogyakarta/Surakarta** (12-14 hrs) US$18 and **Padang** (32 hrs) US$36.

Car hire
Most international companies strongly recommend a driver and local expats believe it is pure madness to attempt tackling the streets of Jakarta oneself. Visitors do, though, and survive. Cars with driver can be hired by the day for about US$65. **Avis**, Jln Diponegoro 25, T021 314 2900, also desks at Soekarno-Hatta Airport and the Borobudur Intercontinental Hotel. **Bluebird**, Jln Hos, Cokroaminoto T021 794 4444. **National**, Kartika Plaza Hotel, Jln MH Thamrin 10, T021 333423/314 3423. **Toyota Rentacar**, Jln Gaya Motor 111/3, Sunter 11, T021 650 6565.

Minibus
Also known as Travels. Door-to-door services are offered by **4848**, Jln Prapatan 34, T021 364 4488, and **Media Taxi**, Jln Johar 15, T021 314 0343. Fares to **Bandung** are US$8 and to **Yogya** US$19. Bear it mind that it can take an excruciating amount of time to pick people up in a city of Jakarta's size, and then there is the traffic to contend with, making this a more stressful and less scenic option than the train ride.

Taxi
This is the most comfortable and convenient way to get around the city. There are numerous companies in Jakarta. **Blue Bird**, T021 7917 1234/794 1234, www.bluebird group.com, is the only company worth using. They can be distinguished by the large Blue Bird Taxi sticker on the windscreen. There are plenty of imitators who have taken to painting their taxis

blue, and whose drivers will try to hustle as much as they can. Flag fall is 6000Rp and 3000Rp for each subsequent km (after the first). Blue Birds can be found outside most major hotels, shopping malls and condo complexes. Tipping is normal, so round up to the nearest 1000Rp if you wish.

Train
Jakarta has 6 railway stations, which are more central than the bus stations. The main station is **Gambir**, on the east side of Merdeka Square (Jln Merdeka Timur). There is an English-speaking information service that advises on timetables and costs, T021 692 9194. Regular connections with **Bogor** (1 hr 20 mins) economy class only, 2500Rp, or the non-stop a/c **Pakuan Express** trains (50 mins) from 0730-1640, 11,000Rp.

For **Bandung**, (2½ hrs) there are the useful **Parahiyangan** trains, departing 6 times a day from Gambir (*bisnis* 30,000Rp/*eksekutif* 60,000Rp). For **Yogyakarta** (8 hrs) there is the **Taksaka**, 2 a day (*eksekutif* US$24). The *eksekutif*-only **Argo Lawu** departs at 2000 and calls in at Yogya before **Surakarta (Solo)** at 0430 (US$25 for either city). The **Argo Dwipangga** does the same trip departing at 0800 and arriving at **Solo** at 1606 (US$24).

There are numerous trains to **Surabaya** (10 hrs) including the **Argo Anggrek**, 2 daily at 0930 (arrives at 1730) and 2130 (arrives at 0730) on *eksekutif* class for US$31.

There is 1 daily train to **Malang**, the Gajayana departing at 1730 and arriving the following morning at 0859, US$35.

Those travelling to **Bogor** and staying in Jln Jaksa or Jln Wahid Hasyim will find it more convenient to jump on a *Pakuan Ekspres* train departing from **Gongdangdia** station, a 10-min walk from the southern end of Jln Jaksa.

Pulau Seribu *p29*
Air
There is an airstrip on Pulau Panjang. The trip takes 25 mins from **Jakarta**. Boat transfers to other islands.

Boat

A regular ferry service goes to **Onrust** and **Bidadari**, leaving Marina Jaya at Ancol at 0700 and returning from the islands at 1430. The journey takes 30 mins-1 hr. If you do not want to take the package option, then go to either Onrust or Bidadari and find a fisherman to take you out for the day to explore the outer islands. It should cost around US$50. Most of the resorts have their own boats, which pick up from Ancol in the mornings. People on day trips can also take these boats.

Krakatau *p29*
Boat

It may be possible to charter boats from Anyer, Carita and Labuan. Locals have gained a reputation for overcharging and then providing unseaworthy boats. (It is said that 2 Californian women spent 3 weeks drifting in the Sunda Strait, living on sea water and toothpaste, before being washed ashore near Bengkulu in West Sumatra.) A 2-engine speed boat suitable for 6-8 people should cost US$150-200. Bargain hard, and make sure you see the boat before handing over any cash. The boatsmen on the beach outside the Mutiara Carita Hotel in Labuan near Carita have a good range of vessels.

ℹ️ Directory

Jakarta *p23, maps p23, p24 and p27*
Banks Most of the larger hotels will have money-changing facilities, and banks and money changers can be found throughout the city centre; for example, in shopping centres. Jln Jaksa also has many money changers, with competition keeping the rate good. Useful banks for visitors include **BNI** and **Lippo Bank** (both with ATMs accepting Visa and MasterCard) on Jln Kebon Sirih. There are ATMs all over the city. Also a money changer with fair rates on the 1st floor of **Sarinah** department store.
Embassies and consulates Austria, Jln Diponegoro 44, T021 338090, auambjak@

rad.net.id. **Australia**, Jln HR Rasuna Said Kav C 15-16, T021 2550 5555, www.austembjak. or.id. **Belgium**, (in Deutsche Bank Building, 16th floor), Jln Imam Bonjol 80, T021 316 2030, jakarta@diplobel.org. **Cambodia**, Jln Kintamani Raya C-15 no 33, T021 574 1437. **Canada**, World Trade Centre, 6th floor, Jln Jend. Sudirman Kav 29, T021 2550 7800, www.geo.international.gc.ca/asia/jakarta/. **Denmark**, Menara Rajawali, 25th floor, Jln Mega Kuningan, T021 576 1478, www. ambjakarta.um.dk. **France**, Jln MH Thamrin 20, T021 3142807, www.ambafrance-id.org. **Germany**, Jln MH Thamrin 1, T021 390 1750, www.jakarta.diplo.de/. **Italy**, Jln Diponegoro 45, T021 337445, www.ambjakarta.esteri. it. **Laos**, Jln Patra Kuningan XIV No 1A, T021 522 9602. **Netherlands**, Jln HR Rasuna Said Kav S3, T021 525 1515, www.indonesia. nlembassy.org. **New Zealand**, Gedung BRI II, 23rd floor, Jln Jend Sudirman 44-46, T021 570 9460, www.nzembassy.com. **Norway**, Menara Rajawali, 25th floor, Kawasan Mega Kuningan Lot 5.1, T021 576 1523, www.norway.or.id. **Philippines**, Jln Imam Bonjol 6-8, T021 315 5118, phjkt@ indo.net.id. **Singapore**, Jln HR Rasuna Said Block X, Kav 2, T021 520 1489, www.mfa. gov.sg/jkt/main.html. **Spain**, Jln H Agus Salim 61, T021 335 0771, embespid@mail. mae.es. **Sweden**, Menara Rajawali, 9th floor, Jln Mega Kuningan Lot 5.1, Kawasan Mega Kuningan, T021 2553 5900, www. swedenabroad.com/jakarta. **Switzerland**, Jln HR Rasuna Said Block X, 3/2, T021 525 6061, www.eda.admin.ch. **UK**, Jln MH Thamrin 75, T021 2356 5200, ukinindonesia.fco.gov. uk/en. **USA**, Jln Medan Merdeka Selatan 5, T021 3435 9000, www.usembassyjakarta. org. **Vietnam**, Jln Teuku Umar 25, T021 910 0163. **Emergencies** 24-hr emergency ambulance service: T118. **Police**: 24-hr emergency T110, Jln Jend Sudirman 45, T021 523 4333. Tourist Police, Jakarta Theatre Building, Jln MH Thamrin 9, T021 566000. **Immigration** Central Immigration, Jln Terminal 2, Cengkareng (near the airport) T021 550 7233. Kemayoran,

Jln Merpati Kemayoran 3, T021 654 1209. Also an office on Jln Rasuna Said, T021 525 3004. These places will extend visas, but get there at 0800 prompt. **Internet** A good internet café is along Jln Jaksa, which provides free drinks for its users and travel services. **Medical services** Clinics: Global Doctor, Jln Kemang Raya 87, T021 719 4565, www.globaldoctorjakarta.com, 24-hr. English-speaking doctors at reasonable rates (US$19 for consultation plus treatment costs). Also **SOS Medika Klinik**, Jln Puri Sakti 10, T021 750 5973, www.sos-bali.com/sos-medika-cipete.php, 24 hr. **Hospitals:** **RS Jakarta**, Jln Jend Sudirman Kav 49, T021 573 2241. **RS MMC Kuningan**, Jln HR Rasuna Said KC21, T021 520 3435 (24-hr emergency room). **Pharmacy: Guardian Pharmacy**, Plaza Indonesia, Pondok Indah Mall or Blok M Plaza. There are a couple of pharmacies on Jln Wahid Hasyim. **Post office** Jln Pos Utara 2, Pasar Baru, or access from Jln Lapangan Banteng, Poste Restante open Mon-Fri 0800-1600, Sat 0800-1300. **Telephone** Telkom, Jakarta Theatre Building, Jln M H Thamrin 81. Open every day, 24 hrs. Numerous **Warpostel** and other telephone offices dotted around.

Bogor

Bogor is centred on the lush botanical gardens, with views over red-tiled roofs stacked one on top of the other and toppling down to the Ciliwung River, which runs through the middle of the town. The Ciliwung, which has cut a deep gorge, has also become a convenient place to discard rubbish, marring some of the views in the process. The town has a large Christian community and a surprising number of Western fast-food outlets and department stores. These serve the population of wealthy Indonesians who live here and commute into Jakarta. A scattering of old colonial buildings is still to be found around town – for instance, set back from the road on Jalan Suryakencana.

The town lies 290 m above sea level in an upland valley, surrounded by Gunungs Salak, Pangrango and Gede. Average temperatures are a pleasant 26°C, significantly cooler than Jakarta, but rainfall is the highest in Java at 3000-4000 mm per year. The Dutch, quite literally sick to death of the heat, humidity and the swampy conditions of Jakarta, developed Bogor as a hill retreat.

Ins and outs → *Phone code: 0251.*

Getting there

Bogor is just 60 km south of Jakarta and with a fast toll road is easily reached on a day trip from the capital. However, it is worth staying here for longer than just a few hours. Bogor is a thriving commuter town and, for many, the first stop from the airport for tourists who only want to see Jakarta on day trips from Bogor (rather than the other way around). The bus station is south of the famous botanical gardens, a longish walk or short *angkot* ride from the town centre, and there are frequent connections with Jakarta's Kampung Rambutan terminal and Soekarno-Hatta International Airport. There are also buses on to Bandung via the Puncak Pass (three hours) and further afield to Yogya, Solo and Bali. The train station is close to the town and there are regular connections with Jakarta's Gambir, Gongdangdia (for Jalan Jaksa and Jalan Wahid Hasyim) and Kota stations. It is best to avoid visiting at weekends as the roads get jammed due to the influx of oxygen-starved visitors from Jakarta gasping for fresh air. ▸▸ *See Transport, page 46.*

Getting around

Bogor is a small town and because it is much cooler here than Jakarta, walking is pleasant, but there are plenty of useful *angkot* routes. Bogor's **tourist office** ⓘ *T0251 836 3433, daily 0900-1700,* is easy to miss, in the bizarre Taman Topi complex on Jalan Kapten Muslihat.

The staff are helpful and have a good map as well as tips on the city. They arrange a number of interesting tours around West Java, and up to the summit of Gunung Salak.

Sights → *For listings, see pages 44-47.*

Botanical gardens (Kebun Raya)
ⓘ *T0251 832 2187, www.bogorbotanicgardens.org, daily 0800-1700, 9500Rp.*
The superb botanical gardens dominate the centre of the city, covering an immense 87 ha and housing 2735 plant species. The gardens are thought to have been established under the instructions of Sir Stamford Raffles. Certainly, Raffles was a keen botanist; however, it was the Dutch Governor-General Van der Capellen who commissioned the transformation of the gardens into arguably the finest in Asia. The botanist Professor Reinhardt, from Kew Gardens in England, undertook the major portion of the work in 1817. The gardens became world renowned for their research into the cash crops of the region (tea, rubber, coffee, tobacco and chinchona – from the bark of which quinine is derived). The giant water lily, as well as a variety of orchids, palms and bamboos, can be seen. It used to be possible to see the giant Rafflesia flower, but it has now died.

Presidential Palace (Istana Bogor)
ⓘ *Those planning to visit the Istana Bogor must think ahead, only groups of 30 or more are admitted after permission has been secured through the Istana or the tourist office at least a week ahead of the planned visit, guests must be formally dressed and children under 10 are not admitted because of the value and fragility of the objects; if visitors can meet all these requirements they deserve a prize. In Jakarta, applications can be made through the Sekretariat Negara, on Jln Veteran 16, www.setneg.go.id.*
Deer graze in front of the imposing Presidential Palace or Istana Bogor, which lies within the botanical gardens, directly north of the main gates (there is also an entrance on Jalan Ir H Juanda). The palace was a particular favourite of President Sukarno and contains a large collection of his paintings, sculptures and ceramics (he had a passion for the female nude). Sukarno lived here under 'house arrest' from 1967 until his death in 1970. Today, it is used as a guesthouse for important visitors and high-level meetings.

Museums
The **Zoological Museum** ⓘ *daily 0800-1700,* is on the left of the entrance to the botanical gardens and was founded in 1894. It contains an extensive collection of stuffed, dried and otherwise preserved fauna (over 15,000 species), of which only a small proportion is on show at any one time. The museum also has a library. There is a **Herbarium** ⓘ *Mon-Thu 0800-1330 and Fri 0800-1000, 2000Rp,* associated with the botanical gardens, on Jalan Ir H Juanda, across the road from the west gate to the gardens. It is said to have a collection of two million specimens, which seems suspiciously inflated.

Markets
Jalan Otista (also known as Otto Iskandardinata) is a road running along the south edge of the botanical gardens. The street is lined with stalls selling fruit, rabbits (not to eat), some batik, children's clothes and unnecessary plastic objects. The main market area is along **Jalan Dewi Sartika**, where stalls, hawkers, shoppers, and angkots struggle for space. It's a fascinating area to walk around, absorb the atmosphere and people-watch.

Gong foundry

ⓘ *Jln Pancasan 17, T0251 832 4132, near the river and southeast of the botanical gardens.*
The gong foundry is one of the few foundries left in Indonesia – on one side of the street is the foundry, and on the other the gong stands are carved from wood. Visitors can watch metalsmiths making gongs in the traditional manner – a process that takes between one and three days per gong. The factory is about a 35-minute walk southeast from the town centre. Walk south down Jalan Empang and then turn right onto Jalan Pahlawan. Next door to the foundry, in addition to selling gongs, traditional puppets of high quality are on offer – and at far lower prices than in Jakarta. About 200 m on from the gong foundry is a small **tofu factory**, a fascinating insight into the simple process of tofu making. Fresh tofu is sold to local villages. Enday Media, a *wayang golek* puppet maker, has his home and **factory** ⓘ *Kampung Sirnagalih 60, T0251 835 8808,* and offers *wayang* shows to groups. Visits can be arranged through the tourist office or through Selfi at Abu Pensione.

Jalan Batutulis

ⓘ *Admission by donation, daily 0800-1600, take an Angkutan (Green Colt) No 02.*
A **batutulis** (inscribed stone), dating from the 16th century and erected by one of the sons of a Pajajaran king, is housed in a small shrine 3 km south of town on Jalan Batutulis (which runs off Jalan Bondongon).

Bogor

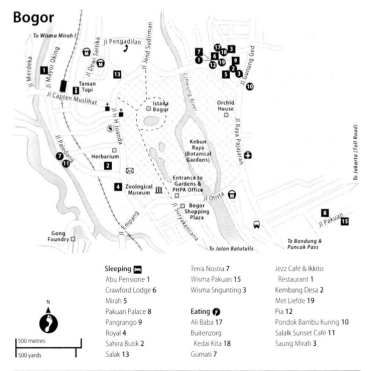

Sleeping 🛏
Abu Pensione 1
Crawford Lodge 6
Mirah 5
Pakuan Palace 8
Pangrango 9
Royal 4
Sahira Butik 2
Salak 13

Terra Nostra 7
Wisma Pakuan 15
Wisma Srigunting 3

Eating 🍴
Ali Baba 17
Buitenzorg
  Kedai Kita 18
Gumati 7

Jezz Café & Ikkito
  Restaurant 1
Kembang Desa 2
Met Liefde 19
Pia 12
Pondok Bambu Kuring 10
Salalk Sunset Café 11
Saung Mirah 3

City tours in and around Bogor

Bogor is a great place to join a tour to absorb some *kampung* ambience, try a bit of Sundanese food and trek off into the untouristed national parks and forests of West Java. Town tours are offered by the tourist office and Selfi at **Abu Pensione** and typically take in the tofu factory, gong foundry, a trip to visit the *wayang golek* puppet maker and try a little local cuisine. The *sop buah* (fruit salad with 12 different locally grown fruits) is a real gastronomic treat and worth ensuring appears on any city tour itinerary. Prices for city tours start at around 225,000Rp per person. Toursts rarely venture into the depths of West Java, a genuine shame given the beauty of the province. Asep (T0818 0809 5615) at the tourist information office in Taman Topi runs a selection of trips into the Gunung Salak and Harimun national parks, offering the chance to spot some wildlife, stay with a local family and climb Gunung Salak. Prices start at 1,200,000Rp per person. He also does longer tours from Bogor ending in Bandung, Pangandaran or Yogya.

Around Bogor

Taman Safari

ⓘ *T0251 825 0000, www.tamansafari.com, daily 0900-1700, 125,000Rp (100,000Rp for children under 5). Take a bus heading for Cisarua and ask to be let off at the turning to the park, motorbike taxis ply the route from the main road to the park gates.*

Just before Cisarua, 2.5 km off the main road, is an open-air safari park. It also houses a mini zoo and offers amusement rides, elephant and horse riding, various animal shows throughout the day, a waterfall, swimming pool, restaurant and camping facilities. There is also a weekend **night safari** ⓘ *Sat 1830-2100, 150,000Rp, under 5s 125,000Rp.*

Bogor listings

For Sleeping and Eating price codes and other relevant information, see pages 9-11.

⊖ Sleeping

Bogor *p41, map p43*

Given its proximity to Jakarta, Bogor is unsurprisingly well endowed with good mid-range and high-end hotels. There are fairly slim pickings at the lower end of the market.

$$$$-$$$ Royal Hotel, Jln Ir H Juanda 16, T0251 834 7123, www.royalhotelbogor.com. Spanking new hotel in the heart of town with rooms offering breathtaking views of the mountains beyond. Rooms are modern, well furnished and have Wi-Fi access. The real draw here is the pool with plenty of loungers from which to watch the sun seting around Gunung Salak. Excellent discounts available. Recommended.

$$$$-$$$ Sahira Butik Hotel, Jln Paledang 53, T0251 832 2413, www.sahirabutikhotel.com. This place has plenty of palatial overtures, friendly staff and fair discounts at weekends. The standard rooms are large and have private balcony. Wi-Fi access available. Pool. Recommended.

$$$ Hotel Salak, Jln Ir H Juanda 8, T0251 835 0400, www.hotelsalak.co.id. Top-notch hotel with formal but comfortable rooms, all carpeted and with Wi-Fi and cable TV. Spa, travel agent, pool and gym.

$$$ Terra Nostra, Jln Salak 8, T0251 833480. Small boutique hotel with a variety of rooms and suites and Balinese flourishes. Some of the suites are sightly on the small side, but could be handy for a family. Wi-Fi offered throughout.

$$$-$$ Hotel Mirah, Jln Pangrongo 9A, T0251 834 8040. The rooms are a little overpriced, given the competition in town.

More expensive ones come with cable TV and are nicely decorated. Further down the price range, rooms are still acceptable, although lose some of the mod cons and become increasingly faded.

$$$-$$ Hotel Pangrango, Jln Pajaran 32, T0251 832 1482, www.hotel-pangrango. co.id. Popular with Indonesian business folk, this 5-storey behemoth has 97 rooms, including budget rooms (with outside bathroom), TV and a/c (centralized-no individual control). The a/c standard rooms are spacious and have TV, fridge and bath. Wi-Fi access in lobby (expensive). Pool.

$$ Crawford Lodge, Jln Pangrango 2, T0251 322429. This place is worth a look for those interested in relieving some 1970s fantasies. It's a little like sleeping in a museum, but the rooms are clean enough and there is an inviting though small pool out the back

$$ Pakuan Palace Hotel, Jln Pakuan 5, T0251 832 3062, hopakuan@indo.net.id. The comfy standard rooms are not bad, with TV, a/c and hot water. Spending a little more will get international cable TV. Pool with outdoor seating. Take angkot No 6 to get here.

$$ Wisma Srigunting, Jln Pangrango 21A, T0251 339 660. Offers 6 rooms set in a spotless though dated and regal family home covered with family photos. The rooms (all a/c) are massive and have fridge and TV, and equally large bathrooms. Some rooms smell a little damp.

$$-$ Abu Pensione, Jln Mayor Oking 15, T0251 832 2893. This place is the best budget bet in town, with a wide variety of clean a/c and fan rooms, some filled with the sound of the gushing river below. The rooms are a little scruffy round the edges and could definitely do with some love The owner, Selfi, is a fountain of local information and great company. She offers excellent tours around town for a glimpse of local life.

$$-$ Wisma Pakuan, Jln Pakuan 12, T0251 319430. Friendly, with helpful staff and large clean a/c and fan rooms with TV around a pleasant garden. Recommended. Take angkot No 6 to get here.

🍴 Eating

Bogor *p41, map p43*
Local specialities include *asinan Bogor* (sliced fruit in sweet water and *tuge goreng*, fried beansprouts served with a spicy chilli sauce). Bogor, like many towns, has a profusion of Padang restaurants, but in this case they are almost all owned by one man and the food is virtually the same, so there is nothing to choose between them gastronomically.

The best food is to be found in the leafy suburb of villas around Jln Pangrango. Prices are fairly high here, but match the setting.

The area around the **Giant** shopping centre on Jln Pajaran has plenty of fast-food options, further down the street towards Jln Otista, there are a few *nasi Padang* restaurants (**Trio** is very popular).

$$$-$$ Kembang Desa, Jln Pangrango 30, T0251 832 9348, www.kembangdesaresto. com. Open 1000-2200. Delightful restaurant serving a range of classical Indonesian dishes from around the archipelago. Highlights include the Tangkapan *ikan di muara* angke (a gorgeous grilled seafood extravaganza) and the rice platters, offering the chance to try different regional dishes. There is a pleasant garden out the back and nightly musical entertainment. We are promised a bar is on the way too. Recommended.

$$$-$$ Saung Mirah, Jln Pangrango 32, T0251 832 7675. Sundanese restaurant offering up tasty *gurame* (grilled carp) and other Sundanese delights in a modern setting.

$$-$ Ali Baba, Jln Pangrango 13, T0251 348111. Open 1000-2200. This is the place to satisfy hummous cravings, with a fair menu of Middle Eastern standards.

$$-$ Buitenzorg Kedai Kita, Jln Pangrango 21, T0251 324160. Open 0800-2300. Relaxed eatery with eclectic menu of pizza, steaks and delicious Sundanese and Javanese dishes. Locals flock here for the coffee menu which includes beans from Sumatra, Timor and Sulawesi.

$$-$ Gumati, Jln Paledang 26, T0251 324318. Open 1000-2300. Brilliant views and superb array of Sundanese food to choose from. There are a few concessions to Western tastes with steaks and some simple pastas. Beautiful views over the mountains from the restaurant. Recommended.

$$-$ Jezz Café and **Ikkito Japanese Restaurant**, Jln Salak 16, T0251 711 1661. Two restaurants on one lot. **Jezz Café** serves cold beer and decent pizza and has pleasant outdoors seating. It's neighbour, **Ikkito**, is well regarded for its *teppanyaki* and *shabu shabu*.

$$-$ Met Liefde, Jln Pangrango 16, T0251 338909. Open 0900-2300 (2400 at weekends). Waitresses in Dutch outfits, displays of clogs and a beautiful garden with outdoor seating. This is a fine spot for a bit of wining and dining for very reasonable prices. The menu is mainly Western, with plenty of Dutch desserts and a good range of juices. Live music at weekends. Recommended.

$ Pia, Jln Pangrango 10, T0251 324169. Open 0800-2200. Pies of every form to consume in a friendly outdoor setting, from chocolate to apple, the house special. There are also plenty of savoury offerings.

$ Pondok Bambu Kuring, Jln Pajajaran 43, T0251 323707. Open 0930-2130. Large restaurant with *lesehan* (low tables) seating. Menu features a lot of good East Javanese seafood dishes with plenty of prawn and squid dishes and some tasty *ikan gurame*.

$ Salak Sunset Café, Jln Paledang 38, T0251 356045. Open 1100-2300. Average Western and Indonesian dishes, with some good snacks including *pisang koreng keju coklat* (fried banana with cheese and chocolate), but the real reason to come here is for the amazing sunset views over the town, perfect for sharing with an icy Bintang.

Shopping

Bogor *p41, map p43*
Batik Batik Semar, Jln Capten Muslihat 7.

Handicrafts Kenari Indah, Jln Pahlawan. Pasar Bogor, Jln Suryakencana.

Market Kebon Kembang, Jln Dewi Sartika. Wayang Golek, Enday Media Kp Sirnagalih 60, T0251 358808.

⛰ Activities and tours

Bogor *p41, map p43*
Tour operators
Maghfiroh, Gedung Alumni IPB, Jln Pajajaran 54, T0251 393234.
Vayatour, Jln Pajajaran 23, T0251 256861, www.vayatour.com. Also **Natatour** upstairs, which can book AirAsia flights.

🚉 Transport

Bogor *p41, map p43*
Bogor is 60 km south of Jakarta. A fast toll road makes the trip to Bogor rapid, though scenically unexciting.

Bus
The station is just off Jln Raya Pajajaran, south from the botanical gardens and opposite the intersection with the toll road from Jakarta. Frequent connections with Jakarta's **Kampung Rambutan** (9000Rp non a/c, 14,000Rp a/c). Bear in mind that Kampung Rambutan is still quite a distance to the centre of Jakarta, making the train trip a much more sensible option. Green angkots from here to the centre of town cost 2500Rp. Regular connections with **Bandung**, via the Puncak Pass, 3 hrs. For travel to Bandung, **Deva Transport**, Jln Taman Yasmin Raya, T0251 753 2582, offers a door-to-door service (3 hrs, 75,000Rp). Phone and book, pay at the end of the journey. Private car companies have also started offering this door-to-door service, with a maximum of 3 passengers. **Bintang Travel**, T0251 915 6699, charges 75,000Rp. This saves the hassle of lugging bags to the bus station and also of getting from the bus station in Bandung into town, which can be a real hassle. For a/c buses to **Yogya**, **Solo** and **Bali**, it is best to go to use one of the well-established bus companies such as **Lorena** (Jln Raya

Tajur 106, T0251 835 6666) and **Pahala Kencana** (Jln Siliwangi 118, Sukasari, T0251 835 3265). Bookings can be made over the phone, or through one of their agents at the bus terminal. Routes include **Denpasar** (27 hrs, US$38), **Yogya/Solo** (15 hrs, US$18), **Surabaya** (19 hrs, US$25), **Padang** (30 hrs, US$38) and **Probolinggo** (21 hrs, US$28). Also connections with **Merak**, **Labuan** and the popular surfer's beach at **Pelabuhanratu**. A very fast, efficient service runs from the Damri Airport Bus Terminal on Jln Pajajaran to Soekarno-Hatta Airport (every 20 mins from 0300-2000, 35,000Rp).

Car hire
Car and driver are available for charter from **Abu Pensione**, Jln Mayor Oking 15.

Cold (Angkutan/angkot)
Omnipresent green machines; there seem to be more of them than there are passengers. Fixed fare of 2500Rp around town; destinations marked on the front. Blue angkots run to out-of-town destinations and are useful for those who fancy heading up to the tea plantations around **Cisarua** in **Puncak**, which have spectacular views and cool, fresh air.

Train
The station (a colonial building) is northwest of the botanical gardens on Jln Rajapermas, also known as Jln Stasiun. Regular connections every 30 mins or so with **Jakarta's** Gambir station. The uncomfortable economy trains take around 1hr 20 mins and cost 2500Rp. Much better are the regular **Pakuan Express** a/c trains that take just under 1 hr and cost 11,000Rp. The first train leaves Bogor at 0540 and the final train out is at 1715. Trains leave from Jakarta's **Kota** station, but also stop at Gambir and sometimes **Gongdangdia** (for Jln Jaksa or Jln Wahid Hasyim) on their way through the capital, en route to Bogor. Note that there are no trains on to Bandung.

ⓘ Directory

Bogor *p41, map p43*
Banks A number on Jln Ir H Juanda and Jln Capten Muslihat, eg BNI 46, Jln Ir H Juanda 42 and **Central Asia**, Jln Ir H Juanda 24. ATMs can be found all over town.
Emergency Police: Jln Capten Muslihat 16. PHKA: Jln Ir H Juanda 9 (also for permits to visit national parks). **Immigration** Jln Jend A Yani 65, T0251 832 2870.
Internet 5000Rp per hr, Blue Corner, Taman Topi, Jln Kapten Muslihat. **Medical services** Hospital: RS PMI Bogor, Jln Pajajaran 80, T0251 839 3030, is run by the Palang Merah Indonesia (Indonesian Red Cross). There is a good selection of specialist doctors here. Pharmacy: Guardian, inside Giant supermarket (2nd floor), Jln Pajajaran. **Post office** Jln Ir H Juanda 3. **Telephone** Wartels all over town.

Bandung

Set in a huge volcanic river basin at an altitude of 768 m and surrounded by mountains, Bandung has one of the most pleasant climates in Java, where the daytime temperature averages 23°C. The town centre is modern, unattractive and overcrowded, and some patience is needed in seeking out the town's main attraction: namely, its fine collection of art-deco architecture, built between 1920 and 1940 when Bandung was the most sophisticated European town of the Dutch East Indies.

The fourth largest city in Indonesia, Bandung is also the capital of the province of West Java. The city has a population of over 2,900,000, with a further 4,000,000 living in the surrounding area, making this one of the most densely populated regions of Java. Such has been the growth of the city that in 1987 its administrative boundaries were extended, doubling the area of the city overnight. Bandung is regarded as the intellectual heart of Java, with over 50 universities and colleges situated in the area. Modern Bandung has the same traffic problems as Jakarta and walking the city is no longer a pleasant stroll; roads are often bumper to bumper with traffic. The heart of the city is looking decidedly rundown nowadays, though those of an artistic orientation should keep an eye out for some genuinely excellent graffiti artwork on shopfronts and walls.

Ins and outs → *Phone code: 022.*

Getting there

Bandung is 187 km southeast of Jakarta, 400 km west of Yogya. The airport is 4 km from town, but most people arrive here by train or bus. The train station is in the centre of town and there are services travelling west to Jakarta and east to Surabaya. Less conveniently located are Bandung's two long-distance bus terminals. The **Leuwi Panjang** terminal is 5 km south of town and serves destinations to the west, including Jakarta. The **Cicaheum** terminal is on the edge of town to the east, and buses from here run to Yogya, Solo, Surabaya and Bali and to towns on Java's north coast including Cirebon and Semarang. Both bus terminals are linked to the centre of town by bemo. The recently completed Cipularang toll road has brought Jakarta within a speedy two hours of Bandung, and at weekends it can seem as if half the capital has arrived there.▸▸ *See Transport, page 57.*

Getting around

Roads are often jammed and the complicated one-way system can be confusing to the uninitiated. However, because Bandung is more than 700 m above sea level, the climate is far cooler than lowland cities like Jakarta and Surabaya and walking is an option. Colts and town buses provide the main means of local transport. Taxis and car hire companies are also found here.

Tourist information

In their office in the northern side of the Masjid Agung on Jalan Asia Afrika, the staff of the **Bandung Visitor Information Centre** ① *T022 420 6644, Mon-Sat 0900-1700 and Sun 0900-1400*, can tell you anything you want to know about Bandung and the surrounding area. The office organizes custom-made tours to suit each visitor's interests; for example,

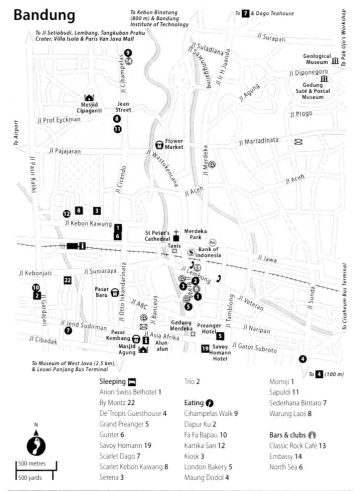

Bandung

Sleeping
Arion Swiss Belhotel 1
By Moritz 22
De'Tropis Guesthouse 4
Grand Preanger 5
Gunter 6
Savoy Homann 19
Scarlet Dago 7
Scarlet Kebon Kawang 8
Serena 3

Trio 2

Eating
Cihampelas Walk 9
Dapur Ku 2
Fa Fa Bapau 10
Kartika Sari 12
Kiosk 3
London Bakery 5
Maung Dodol 4

Momiji 1
Sapuldi 11
Sederhana Bintaro 7
Warung Laos 8

Bars & clubs
Classic Rock Café 13
Embassy 14
North Sea 6

an architectural tour of the town, a pre-historic tour, a trip to the volcanoes, or a tour to visit Sundanese ethnic minorities. Staff are very helpful, particularly the English-speaking Ajid Suryana. There is also an office at the railway station.

Sights → *For listings, see pages 53-58.*

If you want to photograph these buildings, bear in mind that several are occupied by the military and sensitivities are acute.

Colonial art deco

Bandung is recognized as one of three cities in the world with '**tropical art deco**' architecture (the others being Miami, Florida and Napier, New Zealand). The Bandung Society for Heritage Conservation has a register of well over 600 category I and II monuments in Bandung. Of all the art deco architects the one most closely associated with Bandung is Wolff Schoemacher. He graduated with Ed Cuypers from the Delft Technical University in the Netherlands, and then moved to Bandung where he designed hundreds of buildings. In theory, any building over 50 years old is protected and the Mayor of Bandung is said to be appreciative of the need to preserve this heritage. But with the cowboy atmosphere that pervades many other towns and cities, the preservationists will need to be ever watchful.

The most impressive art deco building, lying in the centre of town, is the **Savoy Homann Hotel** on Jalan Asia Afrika, built in 1938 by AF Aalbers and still retaining period furniture and fittings. It has been meticulously renovated at a cost of US$2 million so that visitors can savour a hotel that numbers Charlie Chaplin, Ho Chi Minh and Zhou En-lai among its guests. From the exterior it has been likened to a radio; the interior to an ocean liner. Aalbers is said to have wanted to remind Dutch guests of the ships that brought them to the country. Opposite is the **Preanger Hotel**, built in 1889 but substantially redesigned by Wolff Schoemacher in 1928. The remaining art deco wing faces Jalan Asia Afrika. West on Jalan Asia Afrika is the **Gedung Merdeka** ① *Mon-Fri 0900-1500, free,* also known as the Asia Afrika building. Originally built in 1895, it was completely renovated in 1926 by Wolff Schoemacher, Aalbers and Van Gallen Last, and today houses an exhibition of photographs of the first Non-Aligned Movement conference held here in 1955 (hence the name of the street).

Jalan Braga is often said to be Bandung's colonial heart. Sadly though, most of the original facades have been disfigured or entirely replaced. North of the railway line, also on Jalan Braga, is the **Bank of Indonesia**, designed by Ed Cuypers in the 1920s. Either side are church buildings designed by Schoemacher.

North of the centre

The north suburbs of Bandung are the most attractive part of the city; leafy and green, this is University Land. **Gedung Sate** on Jalan Diponegoro was built in the 1920s and is one of Bandung's more imposing public buildings, with strong geometric lines and a formal garden. Within the building, but rather hidden away, is the **Museum Post and Philately** ① *Jln Cilaki 37, Mon-Fri 0900-1500, free.* Almost opposite is the **Geological Museum** ① *No 57, T022 720 3205, Mon-Thu 0900-1530, Sat-Sun 0900-1330, adult 2000Rp, student 1500Rp,* reputed to be the largest in Southeast Asia. It houses skeletons of pre-historic elephants, rhinos, fossilized trees and a meteor weighing 156 kg that fell on Java in 1884. Most notably, it is home to the skull of 'Java Man'. Unfortunately, there's no information in English. Also north of the city centre on Jalan Taman Sari, the **Bandung Institute of Technology** or ITB was built by Maclaine Pont in 1918 and represents another good example of the architecture of the art deco era.

Off Jalan Taman Sari, just before the ITB travelling north, is the **Kebun Binatang** ① *daily 0800-1600, 10,000Rp, very crowded on Sun and holidays*, Bandung's **zoo** housing Komodo dragons among other beasts. It is set in beautiful surroundings and is well worth a visit. Not far south of the zoo is the rather bizarre '**Jean Street**' on Jalan Cihampelas. Shopkeepers vie for the most elaborate shopfront in an attempt to lure trade. It is a most surreal experience to wander amongst this collection of larger-than-life plaster Rambos, Superman leaping though a wall, and a huge Spiderman casting a web, helicopters, James Bonds and other figures and images, and worth a visit even if you are not intending to shop. There are not just jeans for sale here: all types of clothes, DVDs and merchandise for Bandung's large population of students and trendies are available. The streets are also lined with stalls selling fresh coconuts and durian ice cream – which emits the usual overwhelming smell. To get to the street, take an Angkutan kota running up Jalan Pasir Kaliki and then walk through Jalan Prof Eyckman (Jean Street itself is one-way running south). **Jalan Pasar Selatan** is a more recent imitation of the original, lined with stores selling denim.

South of the centre

South of town, the **Museum of West Java (Negeri Propinsi Jawa Barat)** ① *Mon-Sat 0800-1600,1000Rp*, is on the corner of Jalan Otto Iskandardinata and the ring road. It houses artefacts tracing the development and history of West Java.

One of the minarets of the **Masjid Agung** ① *Jln Jend Sudirman, Sat and Sun only 0900-1700, 2000Rp,* can be climbed for fine views of the city, and the mountains that surround it. Ajid, at the tourist information office (in the north side of the mosque) can also arrange for tours of the huge mosque, but remember to dress conservatively. Men in shorts will not be allowed to enter.

Markets

Like many Indonesian cities, Bandung has a number of markets. **Pasar Kota Kembang** runs along a narrow lane linking Jalan Asia-Afrika and Jalan Dalem Kaum, and specializes in clothes, shoes and accessories. **Pasar Baru** is in Chinatown and is a good place to buy textiles, including batik; the basement houses a vegetable market. **Jalan Pasar Utara** is a food market selling snacks and many West Javanese culinary specialities. Bandung's largest **flower market**, supplied from the many upland nurseries around the city, is on Jalan Wastukencana.

Further north still (7 km) is the **Dago Teahouse** ① *1500Rp daily, early morning until 2200, catch a Dago colt up Jln Ir H Juanda (the colts terminate at Terminal Dago, not far from the Tea House), the Tea House is behind the Pajajaran University housing complex*. It was renovated in 1991, and provides a cultural hall and open-air theatre for evening Sundanese dance performances. There are good views of the city from here and an excellent restaurant. On Saturday nights, Jalan Dago gets crowded with the city's cool young things who hang out snacking, gossiping and listening to loud music around their customized cars.

Around Bandung

Most visitors who venture out of the city travel north into the volcanic **Priangan Highlands** that surround Bandung, to see neat tea plantations, colossal craters and natural hot springs.

Villa Isola

① *Regular minibuses and colts ply this route out of Bandung. Either travel direct from the train station or via Terminal Ledeng at the northern edge of the city*.

This lies on the route north of Jalan Setiabudi, 6 km from the city centre, and is yet another fine art deco building, set on a hill overlooking the city.

Lembang

Lembang, 16 km north of Bandung, is a popular resort town on an upland plateau with restaurants, hotels and pony-drawn carts. It is famous for its pleasant climate and abundance of fresh flowers and fruit. The town can be used as a base to explore the uplands and visit such places as the Tangkuban Prahu Crater and the Ciater Hot Springs (see below). Garden nurseries line the road into Lembang and the town also supports the internationally respected **Bosscha Observatory** ⓘ *visits must be prearranged, regular minibuses connect Lembang with Bandung's Terminal Ledeng, on Jln Dr Setiabudi on the northern edge of the city, to get to Terminal Ledeng, take a colt going up Jln Pasir Kaliki, there are also colts running direct to Lembang from the train station in the centre of town.*

Tangkuban Prahu Crater

ⓘ *Daily 50,000Rp. Guides are unnecessary for the well-defined path to the Domas Crater, but for off-path treks (inadvisable without a guide because of the emissions of sulphurous gases) official guides are available from the tourist information centre at the crater (0700-1700) and cost in the region of 100,000Rp. Beware of the many charlatan guides. Take a bus or colt heading for Subang from either the Leuwi Panjang terminal or from the minibus stop opposite the train station; ask to be dropped off at the entrance to the crater (about 25 km from the city), hitch or walk (3.5 km) from here. At the weekend there are colts that go all the way to the summit.*

Tangkuban Prahu Crater (the capsized boat crater) is one of the most popular tourist sights in the vicinity of Bandung and possibly the most accessible volcanic crater in Indonesia. The route up to the volcano from Lembang passes through rich agricultural land, with terraces of market garden crops clawing their way up the hillsides, chincona trees (the bark is used to produce quinine), teak and wild ginger. The entrance to the 'park' is 9 km from Lembang. The drive from the gate snakes through a forest of giant pines. Some 3 km from the gate is the lower car park (with restaurant and tourist stalls). From here the road continues upwards for another 1 km to the rim of the impressive **Ratu Crater**. Alternatively, there is a footpath from the lower car park to the Ratu Crater (1.5 km), and another from there to the smaller **Domas Crater** (1 km). Another path links the Domas and Ratu Craters (1.2 km). It is also possible to walk all the way round the Ratu Crater. Despite being visited by numerous tour buses and inhabited by large numbers of souvenir sellers, the natural splendour of the volcano makes the trip worthwhile. Ratu rises to an altitude of 1830 m, and the crater drops precipitously from the rim. Bursts of steam and the smell of sulphur bear witness to the volcanic activity latent beneath the surface.

The curious shape of the summit of Tangkuban Prahu has given rise to the Sundanese *Legend of Prince Sangkuriang*, who unknowingly fell in love with his mother, Dayang Sumbi. She tried to prevent their marriage, insisting that her betrothed create a lake and canoe before sunrise on their wedding day. Sangkuriang seemed to be endowed with magical powers and he nearly achieved this impossible task when Dayang Sumbi called upon the gods to hasten the sun to rise, in order to prevent their forbidden union. Sangkuriang was so angry that he kicked his nearly finished canoe, which landed upside down on the horizon, thus creating this silhouette. The wildlife in the surrounding forest includes a small population of native gibbons. At the summit, hawkers sell *angklungs* (hand-held bamboo chimes) to bemused tourists while tapping out *Auld Lang Syne* or *Happy Birthday*. They also vigorously proffer wooden carvings and animals made of small seashells and herbal remedies such as *kayu naga*. This resembles green, hairy twiglets, and is reputedly good for rheumatism and backache. The twiglets are boiled in water and the resultant malodorous brew is drunk.

Ciater Hot Springs
① *T0260 471 700. Open daily 24 hrs. Entrance 16,000Rp, 20,000Rp – 40,000Rp to bathe depending on class. Take a colt or bus towards Subang, ask to be let off at Air Panas Ciater; the hotel and springs are 150 m off the main road.*

Ciater Hot Springs are 6.5 km on from Tangkuban Prahu, the road following the mountainside and winding through tea plantations. There are brilliantly clear hot-water pools and waterfalls here situated on the side of a hill. Unfortunately, the complex is run down.

Ciwidey
① *Regular connections from the Kebon Kelapa terminal, 1½ hrs.*

Ciwidey is a small town about 14 km southwest of Bandung. It is much less touristy and more rural than Ciater – and well worth the effort of getting there. Continuing along the road, up the Ciwidey Valley, the route climbs up past Cimanggu (at the 42 km marker) where there is a small park and hot pools fed from Gunung Patuha (2400 m). The hillsides here are planted with tea bushes. Among the largest estates are the **Rancabali** and **Malabar** estates.

Bandung listings

For Sleeping and Eating price codes and other relevant information, see pages 9-11.

● Sleeping

Bandung *p48, map p49*

Bandung lacks the quality budget accommodation of other Javanese cities, and those in search of clean comfortable digs are advised to spend a little more money here. Many of the city's hotels are scattered conveniently near the train station around Jln Kebonjati and Jln Kebon Kawung. The cost of a room in mid-range and more expensive places increases by around 20% at weekends.

$$$$-$$$ Arion Swiss Belhotel, Jln Otto Iskandarinata 16, T022 424 0000, www. swiss-belhotel.com. Top-class lodgings with tastefully decorated rooms with cable TV, broadband access and all mod cons. Spa, fitness centre and rooftop swimming pool.

$$$$-$$$ Grand Preanger, Jln Asia Afrika 81, T022 423 1631, www.preanger. aerowisata.com. A/c, restaurant (excellent food), pool, original art deco wing (1928), refurbished to a high standard and offering the most interesting rooms, central location, fitness centre, good facilities and well run.

$$$$-$$$ Scarlet Dago, Jln Siliwangi 5, Dago, T022 2500 3000, www.hotelscarlet dago.com. On the edge of town and slightly away from the smog and exhaust fumes is this tasteful modern hotel. Rooms are swanky, the more pricey ones are huge and have massive open balconies. Wi-Fi access in the lobby. Decent weekday promo rates.

$$$ Savoy Homann, Jln Asia Afrika 112, T022 423 2244, www.savoyhomann-hotel. com. The wonderful art deco exterior of this hotel is immediately charming, proving that ageing places of style can be maintained in this country. Rooms are spacious and stylish, and have internet access and cable TV. Discounts available. Recommended.

$$$-$$ Hotel Scarlet Kebon Kawang, Jln H Mesri 11, T022 423 6146. Sprawling mid-range place with clean though slightly dark rooms. Handy for the train station for those arriving late. Good value for the mid-range bracket.

$$$-$$ Hotel Trio, Jln Gardujati 55-61, T022 603 1055, hoteltrio@bdg.centrin.net. id. Crowded with rooms, the **Trio** is popular with Chinese Indonesians and gets very busy at weekends. Rooms are all spotless and well maintained and come with TV and a/c. The more expensive rooms are huge and have a bath and fridge, with plenty of natural light. Pool. Discounts available (20-30%).

$$ De'Tropis Guest House, Jln Windu 6, T021 730 8034, www.detropis.com. Clean and friendly guesthouse set in a neighbourhood compound 20 mins' walk from the town centre. Rooms are well furnished and have cable TV and Wi-Fi access. The staff are friendly and very helpful, making this one of the better mid-range options in town. Decent breakfast and free tea and coffee all day. Recommended.

$$ Hotel Gunter, Jln Otto Iskandarinata 20, T022 420 3763. Faded 1960s hotel with rooms surrounding an immaculate cat-filled garden. Rooms are tatty and have a fair number of spider webs, but bedding is clean. Fan and a/c rooms available, all with TV.

$$ Hotel Serena, Jln Marjuk 4-6, T022 420 4317. This is a good option for those wanting comfort, without being overly extravagant with the pennies. Clean, tiled rooms with a/c, hot water and cable TV are good value here. Wi-Fi access in the lobby. Recommended.

$ By Moritz, Jln Kebon Jati, Luxor Permai 35, T022 420 5788, bymoritz_info@yahoo. com. Things have improved in terms of cleanliness here in recent times, although the place is very quiet and decidedly downmarket. There is a maze-like assortment of very basic fan rooms, some with attached bathroom, also cheaper rooms with common bathroom. The best rooms are the 2 on the roof, with small garden, pleasant seating area and views over the roofs to the south. The downstairs communal area has an assortment of books, TV, simple restaurant and a couple of guitars, occasionally utilized by the friendly staff for yet another rendition of *Hotel California*.

● Eating

Bandung *p48, map p49*
Local dishes including *gorengan* (a form of vegetable-based tempura) *bandrek* and *bajigur* (both drinks made of ginger and sweetened coconut milk respectively) *pecel lele* (fried eels with a piquant sauce) and *comro* (made from cassava and tempe). There are also a large number of bakeries in Bandung, the best selection on Jln Kebon Kawang.

$$ Sapuldi, Jln Chihampelas 105. Open 0900-0000. This place is an oasis of calm off busy Chihampelas, with spacious trationally styled restaurant and a varied menu of Sundanese and regional Indonesian favourites. The best seats are the lesehan seats in the back garden around a fish-filled pond. Recommended.

$$ Momiji, Jln Braga 64, T022 420 3786. Open 1100-2200. Calm and relaxing Japanese restaurant with an extensive menu of sushi, *tempura, udon, tappanyaki* and *bento* boxes. This place is particularly popular with European and East Asian expats at the weekend.

$ Dapur Ku, Jln Lembong 12-18, T022 420 6612. Open 1000-2200. Popular place to try Sundanese cooking, with set meals, or a huge buffet-style selection to choose from. The staff speak good English and can help with deciphering the menu.

$ London Bakery, Jln Braga 37, T022 420 7351. Open 0800-2200. Good selection of coffees, teas, sandwiches and pasta dishes (small portions), with the *Jakarta Post* to linger over. There is an outdoor seating area, although the exhaust fumes are choking.

$ Maung Dodol, Jln Gatot Subroto 28, T022 731 8203. Though slightly out of town, this little eatery has an excellent selection of Sundanese set meals. The *sayur asem* is delicious and the *sambal* firery.

$ Sederhana Bintaro, Jln Jendral Sudirman 111, T022 420 7733. Open 0800-2200. Fans of *nasi Padang* won't want to miss this sparkling restaurant, with an extensive menu of spicy Sumatran favourites and some excellent value set meals. The *sirsak* juice from here is delicious. They can deliver to hotels for free. Recommended.

$ The Kiosk, lining entrance to Braga City Walk, Jln Braga. A line of faux rustic *kaki lima* proffering some excellent value local cuisine in a clean setting. The b*ebek van java* looks promising.

$ Warung Laos, Jln Prof Eyckman 2, T022 203 0516. Mon, Tue 1800-2330, Wed-Sun 1100-2330. Excellent little place just off Jln Cihampelas with pleasant upstairs seating area serving good pizzas, pastas, juices and soups. Recommended.

Chihampelas Walk (see Shopping) has a number of good, clean places (mostly **$**) to eat at in a/c comfort. There are plenty of places to choose from including **Gokana Teppan** (T022 204111), which serves bargain-priced Japanese set meals, and **Cing Wan** (T022 206 1001), which has a menu of Thai and Chinese dishes. Another mall, **Paris Van Java**, has an excellent selection of eateries including Peranakan (Straits Chinese), Japanese and Western cuisine. It is beautifully lit up at night and gets very busy

Jln Gardajati has a selection of Chinese restaurants. **Mei Hwa** and **Red Top** (open for lunch and dinner) are worth investigating.

Bakeries

Fa Fa Bapau, Jln Gardajati 63, T022 607008. Open 0800-2100. Has a fine selection of Chinese buns, filled with pork and spices, or sweet ones with red bean paste. head here for something a little different.

Kartika Sari, Jln Haji Akbar 4, T022 423 1355. Daily 0600-1900. A popular bakery that gets rammed with salivating customers at the weekend. They come for the signature *pisang molan* (pastries filled with banana and cheese), which fly off the shelf.

La Patisserie, in the Grand Preanger (see Sleeping). Open 0800-2100. Has some very naughty chocolate delights, cheesecake, and handy takeaway lasagne and pizza.

Foodstalls

Probably the best are down a tiny alley off Jln Bungsu, near the **Puri Nas Bakery** (open 1730 onwards). Stalls are also on Jln Merdeka, Jln Martadinata, Jln Diponegoro (near the RRI building), Jln Cikapundung Barat and Jln Dalem Kaum, west of the Alun-alun Lor. Most are night stalls only.

Bars and clubs

Bandung *p48, map p49*
Bandung has a great array of bars, pubs and clubs, with good bands and atmosphere.

Jln Braga is a good place to start with a number of bars (many of the somewhat seedy variety), and gets lively in the evenings. Places worth checking out include **Roompoet**, **North Sea Bar**, and **Violet**. Bars open in the late afternoon and close around 0200.

Classic Rock Café, Jln Lembong 1, T022 420 7982. Open 1200-0200. A fun venue covered with rock memorabilia, which has brilliant guitar door handles. Local musicians come to play classic covers and Indonesian rock in the evenings to a lively crowd. Rock music can also be found at **The Rock Café Lounge and Club** on Jln Dr Junjuan 153.

Embassy Score, Cihampelas Walk 160, T022 206 1156. Daily 2200-0600. Renowned club that plays trance and techno to a cool crowd, and attracts some of the nation's best DJs.

Entertainment

Bandung *p48, map p49*
The entertainment schedule is very changeable in Bandung. It is imperative that you check at the tourist information office before you head anywhere.

Adu domba (ram fights)

Ram fights are held most Sundays at **Ranca Buni**, near Ledeng, north of the city on Jln Setiabudi. Get there by taking a Lembung bus to Ledung terminal; walk down Jln

Sersan Bejuri then turn left; there will be many helpful locals around to ask if you get lost. Closer to town, *Adu domba* can be seen on the first Sunday of the month at **Baba Kansiliwangi**. This is within walking distance of the zoo, to the north of the city

Angklung (hand-held bamboo chimes)
Performances are held at **Pak Udjo's workshop**, Jln Padasuka 118 (8 km northeast of the town centre), 1530-1730, 80,000Rp. Take a Cicaheum colt and get off at the intersection with Jln Padasuka, near the Cicaheum bus station. Pak Udjo's workshop is a 7-min walk, on the right-hand side of the street.

Cinema
Blitz Mulitplex, at Paris Van Java, Jln Sukajadi 137-139, T022 8206 3630. Shows all the latest English-language blockbusters, and has very comfy seats, all for between 20,000Rp to 35,000Rp. Recommended.

Cultural shows
Dago Teahouse (see page 51), open stage Sat evenings, free (buy a drink). Sundanese dance and alternative music performances.
Jln Naripan 7, dance rehearsals.
Rumentiang Siang, Jln Barangsiang 1 (near Jln A Yani), T022 423 3562. This is the place to go for performance of Jaipongan (Sundanese dance), epic *wayang golek* shows, *ketoprak* (traditional theatre).
STSI (Institute of Fine Arts), Jln Buah Batu, T022 731 4982. Performances and rehearsals of Sundanese dance, theatre and music.

⊙ Shopping

Bandung *p48, map p49*
Art galleries Bandung is viewed as a centre for Indonesian arts and there are a number of galleries in town exhibiting work by promising young Indonesians. There are

a few galleries along Jln Braga including: **Barli**, Jln Prof Dr Sutami 91, T022 201 1898, Mon-Sat 0900-1700, collection of traditional and contemporary art; **Bunga Art Gallery**, Jln Braga 41, T022 731 0960, daily 0900-1800; **Jalu Braga**, Jln Braga 29, daily 0700-2200; and **Taman Budya Jawa Barat**, Jln Bukit Dago Selatan 53, T022 250 5364, Mon-Sat 0900-2200, Sundanese art, occasional performances.

Batik Batik Abstrak, Jln Tirtasari 9, T081 5628 1358. Funky and super-modern batik designs.

Books Branch of QB Books on Jln Setiabudi to the north of town. Daily 0900-2100. Good selection of English-language books and a relaxed café with Wi-Fi access.

Distros Taken from the Indonesian word *distribusi* (distribution), distros are a fashion phenomenon in Bandung that has spread elsewhere in Indonesia, notably to posh south Jakarta. These independent shops are run as cooperatives and act as distributing agents for local designers who do not have the means or desire to produce mass goods in a factory. The T-shirts and other clothing produced is therefore original and rare. Distros can be grungy places, with graffiti-covered walls and hard rock soundtracks, all adding to their underground charm. As with all things that are cool, there is some fear of distros becoming too mainstream, and losing the cooperative spirit that make them so popular. Bandung has over 200. If you're in the market for a cool T-shirt, check out the following distros, all on Jln Trunojoyo: **Blackjack**, **Screamous**, **Achtung** and **Cosmic**.

Handicrafts Pa Aming, Jln M Ramdhan 4; and **Pak Ruchiyat**, Jln Pangarang Bawah IV No 78/17B (behind No 20 in the alleyway). Both are workshops where you can also buy and the latter is reputed to sell perhaps the finest worked examples. **Pak Ruchiyat** has over 35 years' experience; note that prices are fixed. Shops along Jln Braga sell puppets. **Cupumanik**, Jln Haji Akbar, Mon-Sat 0900-1600. Collection of locally made masks, puppets and handicrafts. **Eddy Noor Gallery**, Jln Villa Bandung Indah, T022 707 1135. Beautiful painted glass exhibition by a local artist.

Shopping malls Chihampelas Walk, Jln Chihampelas 160, T022 206 1122. Brand-name goods in a clean a/c environment. Good for taking a breather from manic Jeans St shopping.

Supermarket Carrefour, Braga Walk, daily 1000-2200, is a good place to stock up on necessities. You can also find a few cafés and fast-food outlets here.

▲ Activities and tours

Bandung *p48, map p49*
Tour operators
Kangaroo Travel and Tours, Hotel Perdana Wisata, Jln Jebdral Sudirman 66-68, T022 420 0334.
Satriavi, Grand Hotel Preanger, Jln Asia Afrika 81, T022 420 3657, www.aerowisata.co.id.

Tours
The tourist office on Jln Asia Afrika will organize tours in and around town, as will many of the travel agents (depending on season and demand). Typical tours visit the Tangkuban Prahu crater and Ciater hot springs (5 hrs, US$40 per person), architecturally interesting buildings around town (3 hrs, US$12 per person) and an angklung music performance, plus traditional Sundanese dancing (3 hrs, US$10 per person).
By Moritz (see Sleeping, page 54) organize day trips to Mt Papandayan, with a guide leading visitors all over the mountain, and a bath in a sulphur spring. They also have trips to Ciwidey, to see the tea plantations, Cibuni crater and Danau

Patenggang. All tours from By Moritz cost around US$45 per person, but prices are highly negotiable.

Walks
The Bandung tourist office has identified a number of walks in the city through the Central Business District (CBD), Chinatown and elsewhere. For maps and further information contact the tourist office – good background information on buildings and the city's history is available.

⊖ Transport

Bandung *p48, map p49*
Most roads in the centre of town are one-way. This, coupled with the dense traffic, makes it quite a struggle getting around town. Bandung must have more orange-suited traffic wardens than any other town on Java, ready to direct traffic dangerously (and collect their 300Rp *parkir*). Colts (Angkutan kota) charge 3000Rp for journeys around town and up to 5000Rp for longer journeys. They can be found at the station on Jln Kebonjati.

Air
Bandung's **airport** is 4 km from the city, T022 604 1313. Fixed price transport to town by taxi, US$7. **AirAsia** flies to **KL**, **Singapore**, **Denpasar**, **Medan** and **Pekanbaru**. Malaysian Airlines has flights to **KL** and **JB**. Merpati flies to **Batam**, **Yogyakarta**, **Surabaya**, **Denpasar** and **Kupang**. There are daily flights to **Jakarta** on Garuda and Wings Air. Sriwijaya flies to **Surabaya**. Susi Air flies daily to **Pangandaran** and **Jakarta** (**Halim**) in their tiny 12-seater Cessna.
   Airline offices Garuda, Jln Asia Afrika 118, T022 421 7747. **Merpati**, Jln Kebon Kawung 16, T022 4230 3180. Sirwaijaya, Jln Burangrang, T022 733 4026. **Susi Air** (book through Jakarta office: Susi Air Jakarta, BNI 46 Building 32nd floor, Jln Sudirman Kav I, T021 3929 726.

Bus

Local City buses go north–south or east–west; west on Jln Asia Afrika, east on Jln Kebonjati (beware that Nos 9 and 11 stop at 2100) south on Jln Otto Iskandarinata, north on Jln Astanaanyar, 3000Rp.

Long distance Bandung has 2 long-distance bus terminals: for destinations to the west is the **Leuwi Panjang** terminal, 5 km south of the city centre on Jln Soekarno-Hatta. Serves destinations including **Jakarta** (Kampung Rambutan terminal), **Bogor** and **Sumatra**. Terminal **Cicaheum** on Jln Jend A Yani (40,000Rp taxi ride from city centre) serves destinations to the east and north, including **Yogya**, **Solo**, **Surabaya**, **Garut**, There are also direct buses to **Pangandaran** (60,000Rp).

To avoid the hassle of going to the terminals, it is best to book bus tickets through **Pahala Kencana** (Jln Kebonjati, T022 42) or **Kramat Jati** (Jln Kebonjati (T022 420085). Both companies have buses departing from their offices to **Denpasar** (24 hrs, US$32), **Probolinggo** (19 hrs, US$30), **Surabaya** (19 hrs, US$17.50) **Yogya** and **Solo** (8-9 hrs, US$12.50).

Minibus Phone to make a booking, or get the hotel staff to do it for you, and pay when you have reached your destination. **4848**, T022 422 4848, has door-to-door services to **Jakarta** (US$10), and **Pangandaran** (US$8). **Sarum Hari**, T022 607 7065, also offers 2 daily connections with Pangandaran at 0600 and 1300 (US$8), **Deva Travel**, Jln Jend. A Ayani 810, T022 720 0679, offers 2 daily door-to-door services to **Bogor** (0400, 0900, US$8). **Primajasa**, T022 607 3992, has minibuses departing hourly from 0800-2100 from Bandung Super Mall to Jakarta's **Soekarno-Hatta** airport (3 hrs, US$9). **Cipaganti**, T022 426 4525, also offers this service as well as trips to various suburbs in the capital.

Car hire

Mulia Car Rental, Batununggal Indah 39, T081 201 5606, www.muliarental.com.
Total Car Rental, Jln Jajaway Dago Atas 12A, T022 8252 0044, www.rental.total.or.id.

Taxi

Taxis are notorious for rip-offs.
The only company worth using is
Blue Bird, T022 756 1234.

Train

The station is behind the bemo station, on Jln Stasion Barat and has a helpful information line with English-speaking staff (T022 426 6383). Regular connections with **Jakarta's** Jatinegara and Gambir stations. The best service is the **Parahiyangan** with 6 daily departures to **Gambir** taking 2½ hrs (*bisnis* US$3/*eksekutif* US$6). The **Lodaya** calls in at **Tasikmalaya**, Banjar (for **Pangandaran**), **Yogya** and **Solo** (*bisnis* US$11/*eksekutif* US$18). For **Surabaya**, hop on the daily **Argo Wilis** (*eksekutif* US$23).

Directory

Bandung *p48, map p49*
Banks There are banks all over Bandung. BNI, Jln Braga 23; HSBC, corner of Jln Tamblong and Jln Asia Afrika. ATMs can be found along all commercial streets, particularly Jln Braga, Jln Cihampelas, Jln Jendral Sudirman and Jln Asia Afrika. Money changers: VIT Jln Cihampelas, in a small booth opposite Adventist Hospital. Aneka Artha Mas, Jln Naripan 43, T022 424 1204. **Internet** One Byte, Jln Cihmapelas 74, T022 426 3992, 5000Rp per hr. **Medical services** Chemist: Ratu Farma, Jln Kebonjati 106, T022 439892. Hospital: Adventist Hospital, Jln Cihampelas 161, T022 203 4386.
Post office Jln Asia Afrika 49, corner of Jln Asia Afrika and Jln Banceuy, Poste Restante available. **Telephone** Wartel, Jln Asia Afrika (opposite Savoy Homann Hotel), for international calls and fax.

Pangandaran

Pangandaran is situated on the neck of a narrow isthmus and offers some of the best beaches on the south coast of Java. Originally a fishing village, many of the local people now derive their livelihoods from tourism. At weekends, during peak season, the town is crowded with Indonesian tourists; out of season, on weekdays, it is like a ghost town and hotel and losmen prices can be bargained down. The high season is June to September, the low season October to March.

On 17 July 2006, Pangandaran was hit by a tsunami. The tidal wave, at least 3 m high, devastated the coastal strip ploughing as far inland as 400 m and washing away hundreds of houses and businesses. Many locals have heartbreaking stories to tell and are trying hard to rebuild their lives, but there is still plenty of evidence of the disaster. The owner of Lotus Wisata, Lia Natalia, whose business was washed away, has an album of photos taken after the tsunami showing the immediate damage.

A visit to Pangandaran is highly recommended as a foil to the beaches of Bali and Thailand. It is a great chance to observe Javanese beach culture without the overload of tie dye and banana pancakes, and the surrounding countryside is truly superlative.

Note Look for the *Jalur Evakuasi* (Evacuation Route) signs around town in the unlikely event of another disaster occurring.

Beaches → *Phone code: 0265. For listings, see pages 61-64.*

ⓘ *Admission to the isthmus is 5000Rp.*

The best beach is on the west side of the isthmus and is named **West Beach** (Pantai Barat). Swimming is not recommended as currents are vicious. Look out for the red flags warning of dangerous areas. Locals seem to ignore the warning signs and there are lines of vendors offering body board rental (25,000Rp an hour) for those who fancy an exhilirating splash about. Souvenir shops line the beachfront and most accommodation is concentrated here. The east side of the isthmus, **East Beach** (Pantai Timur), is less developed; the water is often rough and swimming is poor, sometimes dangerous. Fishermen cast their nets from this shore and land their catches along the beach. Their colourful boats lining the shore are a lovely sight. The fish market is worth a visit in the mornings if you can stand the smell! The **PHKA tourist office** is on the edge of the park at the south end of the isthmus, near East Beach. Lia Natalia at **Lotus Wisata** speaks excellent English and is a good source of local information.

The promontory of the isthmus is the **Penanjung National Park** ① *0700-1730, 7500Rp, guides 100,000Rp for a tour lasting 4 hrs and worth the money*, only half of which is open to tourists. On both the east and west sides of the promontory are white-sand beaches. It is possible to walk the 10 km around the shoreline of the peninsula, or hike through the jungle that is said to support small populations of buffalo, deer, tapirs, civet cats, porcupines and hornbills, although how they tolerate the herds of tourists is a mystery. The Rafflesia flower can apparently be seen here in season. The park also has some limestone caves.

Around Pangandaran

Batu Karas ① *get here by hired motorbike or take a bemo to Cijulang, then hop on an ojek for the last 10 km to the beach from the main road*, is popular with surfers.

Green Canyon ① *take a minibus from Pangandaran to Cijulang, and then an ojek from there, most hotels run tours to the canyon, which will also include a full day visit to local farming and craft industries; alternatively, visit the tourist information office for cheaper, good tours, starting at 150,000Rp per person*, is a very popular day trip. Boat hire is regulated and costs 80,000Rp per *prahu* (which seat up to eight people). Travelling upriver, the foliage becomes denser and the rocks close in, until you find yourself entering a canyon. After 15-20 minutes, the boat's path is blocked by rocks. There is a large plunge pool here, with swimming and rubber rings for hire. The best time to visit is during the week, as it gets crowded at weekends and holidays; a recommended trip.

Pangandaran

Sleeping 🛏		Eating 🍴	
Adam's Homestay 1	Nyuir Resort 5	Chez Mama Cilacap 1	Only One Resto 5
Laut Biru 3	Pondok Daun 8	Eka Bamboo Cafe 2	Pasar Ikan 3
Mini Tiga 4	Puri Alam 9	Mungil 4	Relax 6
	Sandaan 10		

Parigi Bay ① *regular buses run from Pangandaran bus station on Jln Merdeka, ask specifically for a beach, eg Batu Karas, the bus doesn't go all the way – only to the bridge over the Green River (5000Rp); from here you need to hire a motorbike or hitch a lift*, is west of Pangandaran, and offers better and quieter beaches than the isthmus, namely **Batu Hiu**, **Batu Karas** and **Parigi**, and good water for surfing.

A worthwhile alternative to the bus trip back to Banjar is the much more enjoyable ferry journey from Kalipucang to Cilacap (see Transport, page 63). Local trips around the peninsula, stopping to swim or snorkel, can be bargained for with the local fishermen (around US$30). Trips to tiny white-sand islands (infrequently visited and uninhabited) off the peninsula cost about US$35 for a one-hour boat ride, and then you can stay on the island as long as you wish. A trip to **Nusakambangan** is available from Pangandaran (US$30). The island, once forbidden to tourists because of a high-security prison located there, has unspoilt beaches and forests. The prison is considered the highest security jail in the country and has played host to notables including Tommy Soeharto, poet and novelist Pramoedya Ananta Toer and the three Bali bombers – Imam Samudra, Amrozi, and Ali Gufron – who were executed here by firing squad in November 2008.

It's also possible to charter a boat between Kalipucang (Pangandaran's 'port') and Cilicap through the **Anakan Lagoon**, an 'inland' sea. A recommended four-hour journey and a gentle form of transport, the boat sails down the mangrove-clothed Tanduy River, stopping off in various fishing villages, before crossing the lagoon. The Tanduy River marks the border between West Java and Central Java. The last village before the ferry turns into the lagoon, **Majingklak**, is the easternmost village in West Java. The large island bordering the south of the lagoon and protecting it from the Indian Ocean, is **Kampangan Island**. In 1912, the Dutch depopulated the island, resettling three fishing villages, with the intention of making it a prison. The lagoon is one of Indonesia's largest areas of wetland and has a varied water bird population. For keen birdwatchers it is possible to jump ship at one of the fishing villages, sleep in a homestay, and then charter a boat to explore the lagoon early the next morning, before continuing the journey to Cilacap (or vice versa).▸▸ *See Transport, page 63.*

Pangandaran listings

For Sleeping and Eating price codes and other relevant information, see pages 9-11.

● Sleeping

Pangandaran *p59, map p60*
Accommodation is concentrated on the west side of the isthmus – there are around 100 hotels and *losmen*. Rates can be bargained down substantially during low season (Oct-Mar) and weekdays. At Christmas and during Jul and Aug prices rise steeply. Many hotels and guesthouses rent out family rooms–usually 2 double rooms and living area.
$$$ Laut Biru, Jln Embah Jaga Lautan 17-18, T0265 639360, www.lautbiru.com.

Handily located near a good stretch of beach and the entrance to the national park, this place has great facilities, comfortable rooms and good service. Pool. Substantial discounts available.
$$$ Nyuir Resort Hotel, Jln Bulak Laut, T0265 639349, www.nyiurresorthotel.com. Rooms here are overpriced and geared towards package tour groups. However, the hotel has all the trimmings of a resort with a pleasant garden, pool and restaurant.
$$-$ Sandaan, Jln Bulak Laut, T0265 639165. Wide variety of rooms, all of which are clean, and improve dramatically as prices rise. Standards have a/c and TV, but they face a brick wall. The more expensive de luxe

rooms have a pleasant veranda and views of the pool.

$$ Adam's Homestay, Jln Bulak Laut, T0265 639396. Wonderful gardens, with ponds and small streams aplenty. Rooms are huge, and have fridge, a/c and TV. Pool. Recommended.

$$ Pondok Daun, Jln Bulak Laut 74, T0265 639788. Spacious clean rooms all with a/c, TV and outdoor bathroom, in a shady garden with small pool.

$$ Puri Alam, Jln Bulak Laut Depan Pasar Wisata, T0265 631699. The staff here don't speak English but are extraordinarily friendly and make every effort to ensure visitors feel at home. This hotel is covered in greenery further adding to its charms. Good-value spacious rooms, with TV and a/c. Breakfast not included. There is also a huge bungalow on site available for rental at weekends, which would suit a large group. Recommended.

$ Mini Tiga, Jln Bulak Laut, T0265 639436, kalmaja@yahoo.fr. This is prime backpacker territory and a great spot to meet up with fellow travellers and discuss the road ahead. The hotel feels a bit cramped, but has a pleasant café area, clean and simple fan rooms with attached bathroom. Recommended.

🍴 Eating

Pangandaran *p59, map p60*
There are innumerable places to eat, some of which are geared to Western tastes. Not surprisingly, seafood is by far the best bet.

$ Chez Mama Cilacap, Jln Kidang Pananjung, T0265 639098. Open 0730-2300. Excellent place for fresh seafood and breakfast. Also some Western standards. Recommended.

$ Eka Bamboo Café, Jln Bulak Laut, T0818 0974 0899. Open 0800-0100. Good for a cheap breakfast, a late-night beer or to sample some local cuisine including *nasi uduk*. This place has a repuatation as a bit of a party place and is a good spot to socialise.

$ Only One Resto, Jln Bulak Laut, T0265 639969. Open 0700-2300. This comfortable

and popular eatery has sea views, good fresh seafood, and tasty Indonesian cuisine.

$ Pasar Ikan, Jln Talanca. Open 0700-2000. If you only have one night in Pangandaran, this is the place to go. For seafood fans the *pasar ikan* is one of the best places in Java to get the catch of the day with its collection of clean restaurants serving up shark, lobster, jumbo prawns and fish accompanied by gargantuan portions of delicious *sambal kangkung* (water spinach fried with sambal). One of the more popular places is **Sari Melati** (T0265 639735). Recommended.

$ Patisserie, Jln Bulak Laut. Open 0700-2300. Pleasant spot to start the day with beach views, a decent menu of sandwiches and cakes and some Western standard dishes.

$ Restaurant Relax, Jln Bulak Laut 74, T0265 630377. Open 0800-2300. Run by a European woman, this place has delicious fresh brown bread, hard central European cheeses and offers a variety of Western and Indonesian dishes, excellent juices and lassis and some rather tasty cakes in a homely European café-style setting. Those in the mood for something substantial will find solace in the goulash. Recommended.

🍸 Bars and clubs

Pangandaran *p59, map p60*
Pangandaran isn't really a place to go wild, but on Sat nights the town comes alive and it is worth visiting one of the *dangdut* pubs that line the main road.

The Spot, at the **Surya Pesona**, see Sleeping. Open 2000-0100. Down a few bottles of *kratingdaeng* and dance with the local youths to ear-bleeding techno. There are occasional *dangdut* nights here for those in search of something a little more laid-back. Western visitors often congregate at **Only One Resto** or **Bamboo** for a drink and natter.

● Shopping

Pangandaran *p59, map p60*
There is a large **Pasar Wisata** (tourist market)
0800-2100, which is mournfully empty on
weekdays, selling cheap tourist trinkets.
There is also a supermarket on Jln Merdeka,
open 0800-2200.

▲ Activities and tours

Pangandaran *p59, map p60*
Tour operators
There are plenty of unlicensed guides
wandering the streets and hanging out
in cafés looking for business.

Tour agencies organize jungle, boat
(fishing, snorkelling), home industry, village
and other tours. Trips include a 6-hr visit to
Green Canyon (US$15), a jungle tour (US$10)
and many more. All tours include appropriate
entrance fee, guide and lunch on longer
excursions. Most hotels offer tours, and they
can also be booked at **Lotus Wisata** (see
below). Almost every hotel organizes trips
to Yogya and Bandung, etc.

Lotus Wisata, Jln Bulak Laut 2, T0265
639635. Organizes local tours and transport
to and from Pangandaran; recommended.

● Transport

Pangandaran *p59, map p60*
400 km from Jakarta, 129 km from Bandung,
66 km from Banjar and 312 km from Yogya.

Air
Susi Air, www.susiair.com, has daily flights
to **Bandung** and **Jakarta** (Halim). Book
well in advance at travel agents around
town or directly at their office on Jln
Merdeka 31, T0265 639120.

Becak/bike/car/motorbike hire
Becaks and bicycle hire along the beach and
from guesthouses, around US$4 per day.
Lotus Wisata, Jln Bulak Laut 2, T0265 639635.

Rents motorbikes for around US$5 per day
and cars for US$35 for 24 hrs, with a driver.

Boat
A private boat journey between **Kalipucan**
(15 km from Pangandaran; take a local
bus) and **Cilicap** takes 4 hrs. Approaching
Cilacap is LP Nusa Kembangan, Indonesia's
top security prison. The boat docks at **Sleko**,
outside Cilacap. There is currently no public
boat service running; chartering a boat costs
US$50. See also page 61.

Bus
There are 2 stations on Jln Merdeka, north
of the hotels and guesthouses (outside the
main gates). Local bus connections tend
to leave from the station at the eastern
end of Jln Merdeka, not far from the main
intersection before the gate, while express
buses leave from the company terminal
further west along Jln Merdeka. Regular
buses link Pangandaran with **Banjar**
(15,000Rp), from where there are frequent
buses onward to **Jakarta** (7-10 hrs), **Bogor**
(via **Ciawi**), **Bandung** (6 hrs), **Yogya** and
Solo. Jakarta–Banjar buses leave Jakarta's
Cililitan station every hour. There are also
some direct connections with **Jakarta**
(8 hrs) and **Bandung**. Travel agents in town
sell tickets for popular routes. For tickets
to Bandung, head to the **Budimans** office
at the bus terminal from where there are
regular a/c buses (5-6 hrs, US$5).

Minibus An a/c door-to-door service
can be booked at **Lotus Wisata** (see
above) and most guesthouses in town.
Daily departure to **Bandung** (daily at
0600, US$10) and 2 daily departures to
Yogyakarta (departing 0600 and 0700
US$15). Be warned that this minibus service
takes a lot longer than the train and stops
at small villages and towns along the way
to pick people up. Nevertheless, it's a scenic
ride and if you're in no hurry, sit back and
enjoy the views.

Train

No direct trains link Pangandaran with **Jakarta**, **Yogya**, **Bandung** or **Solo**. It is necessary to change in **Banjar**, a small town on the Bandung–Yogya road, and 66 km from Pangandaran. There are a number of cheap *losmen* over the railway bridge from the rail and bus stations in Banjar, for those who arrive too late to make a connection. The train and bus stations are 500 m apart; becaks wait to take travellers between them. Regular connections with **Jakarta** (1 daily, 10 hrs), **Bandung** (6 daily, 5 hrs, *eksekutif* US$19), **Yogya** (2 daily, 5 hrs, *eksekutif* US$18.50) and **Surabaya** to Banjar. Regular buses link Banjar with Pangandaran. Travel agents in Pangandaran sell package bus-train tickets that include pick up from hotel in Pangandaran and train ticket from Banjar. Packages cost around US$30 for an *eksekutif* train ticket to Yogya.

❶ Directory

Pangandaran *p59, map p60*
Banks Bank Rakyat Indonesia and BNI both have branches on Jln Merdeka. There is a BNI ATM on Jln Bulak Laut, opposite the Relax Restaurant. **Lotus Wisata** will change money. **Post office** Jln Kidang Pananjung 111, Poste restante available here. **Telephone** Telkom, Jln Kidang Penanjung, has an international phone service.

Yogyakarta

Yogyakarta (usually shortened to Yogya and pronounced 'Jogja') is the most popular tourist destination in Java. It is a convenient base from which to visit the greatest Buddhist monument in the world – Borobudur – and the equally impressive Hindu temples on the Prambanan Plain. The town itself also has a number of worthwhile attractions: the large walled area of the kraton, with the sultan's palace, the ruined water gardens or 'Taman Sari', and a colourful bird market. Yogya is arguably the cultural capital of Java, and certainly its many private colleges and university attest to its being the island's educational heart, which also accounts for the younger, relatively affluent individuals you will see in the city. For the tourist, it is also one of the best centres for shopping and offers a good range of tourist services, from excellent mid-range accommodation to well-run tour companies.

Yogya is situated at the foot of the volcano Gunung Merapi, which rises to a height of 2911 m, to the north of the city. This peak is viewed as life-giving, and is set in opposition to the sea, which is life-taking and situated to the south. The importance of orientation with relation to Gunung Merapi and the ocean is seen clearly in the structure of the kraton, or sultan's palace.

In late 2010, Mount Merapi, the gorgeous volcano clearly visible from the city on a sunny day, erupted numerous times over the space of a month covering the city in fine white ash. Major damage was done to the villages closer to the volcano with the displacement of over 350,000 people and the deaths of 353 people, many as a result of devastating pyroclastic flows. Flights in and out of the city were cancelled as the authorities declared the eruption the largest since 1870. In December 2010 the eruptions subsided and the alert status was downgraded to level 3. Tourists are now scuttling up the north side of the volcano once again.

Ins and outs → *Phone code: 0274.*

Getting there

Yogyakarta may not be in the top league of Javanese towns by population, but because it is such an important destination for tourists it is well connected. **Adisucipto International Airport** ① *8 km east of town, T0274 486666*, is the nation's fourth busiest and has daily flights from Kuala Lumpur and Singapore (with **AirAsia**) and daily connections with destinations in Java and further afield. The train station is centrally situated on Jalan Pasar Kembang, and there are regular services to Jakarta's Gambir station (565 km), and east to Surabaya (327 km) and frequent departures to Solo. The Umbunharjo long-distance bus terminal is 4 km southeast of the city centre, at the intersection of Jalan Veteran and Jalan Kemerdekaan. Buses of all types depart for most towns in Java and beyond. Agents for tourist buses and minibuses can be found throughout the hotel and *losmen* areas of town and particularly on Jalan Sosrowijayan and Jalan Prawirotoman. ▸▸ *See Transport, page 81.*

Getting around

While Yogya is not a small town by any means, exploring the city on foot, or a combination of foot and becak, is not beyond the realms of possibility. Becaks can be chartered by the hour or by the trip. Town buses (pick up a route map from the tourist office), bemos and colts offer cheaper local transport options. The excellent **TransJogja** bus lines offer fast, clean and efficient transportation around town for a flat fee of 3000Rp. Routes can be found at www.transjogja.com/rute. Note that becak and bemo drivers have an unerring tendency to take their passengers on extended tours of shops and art galleries. Taxis can be chartered by the trip, or by the hour, half-day or day. Self-drive car and motorbike hire is readily available, as are bicycles.

Tourist information

Tourist information office ① *Jln Malioboro 14, T0274 566000, Mon-Thu, Sat 0800-1900, Fri 0800-1800*, offers free maps of the town and environs, information on cultural events, bus routes, etc. There is also a tourist office counter at the railway station and another at the airport.

Sights → *For listings, see pages 74-83.*

Alun-alun Lor

Yogya's main street is Jalan Malioboro, which runs from north to south. At its south end, the street becomes Jalan Jend A Yani and then Jalan Trikora, which leads into the kraton and the grassed square known as the Alun-alun Lor. This square was the site of major events such as tiger and buffalo fights, which were staged here from 1769. A raised stand afforded the sultan and any visiting Dutch dignitaries a good view of the spectacle. The tiger was deemed to represent the foreigner and the buffalo, the Indonesian. Invariably, the buffalo would win the contest – often with some help – but the symbolism was lost on the Dutch. Nonetheless, the unperceptive Dutch still succeeded in dominating Yogya and Indonesia. There are two sacred *waringin* trees (*Ficus benjamina*) in the centre of the square. The *waringin* represents the sky and the square fence or *waringin kurung* surrounding the trees, the earth with its four quarters. At the same time, the tree is said to symbolize chaotic nature, and the fence human order. If you see people blindly stumbling around, don't be alarmed. It's just the locals taking part in Masangin (*masuk antara dua beringin*), a game where they must walk between the two ficus trees blindfolded.

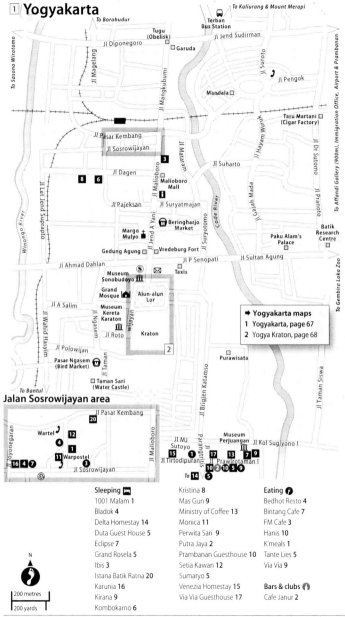

1 Yogyakarta

To Kaliurang & Mount Merapi

To Borobudur

Terban Bus Station

Tugu (Obelisk)

JI Diponegoro

Garuda

JI Jend Sudirman

To Sasono Wirotomo

JI Magelang

JI Suroto

JI Pengok

Mandala

JI Mangkubumi

To Affandi Gallery (900m), Immigration Office, Airport & Prambanan

Taru Martani (Cigar Factory)

JI Pasar Kembang

JI Sosrowijayan

JI Mataram

JI Suharto

JI Hayam Wuruk

JI Dr Sutomo

JI Dagen

3

JI Pranoto

8 6

JI Maliboro

Malioboro Mall

JI Pajeksan

JI Suryatmajan

Margo Mulyo

JI Jend A Yani

Beringharjo Market

Code River

JI Suryotomo

JI Gajah Mada

Paku Alam's Palace

Batik Research Centre

Gedung Agung

Vredeburg Fort

JI P Senopati

JI Sultan Agung

JI Ahmad Dahlan

Taxis

To Gembira Loka Zoo

Museum Sonobudoyo

Grand Mosque

JI A Salim

Alun-alun Lor

JI Wahid Hasyim

Museum Kereta Karaton

JI Nageran

JI Roto

Wijilan

Kraton

➡ Yogyakarta maps
1 Yogyakarta, page 67
2 Yogya Kraton, page 68

JI Polowijan

2

JI Brigjen Katamso

Purawisata

JI Taman Siswa

Pasar Ngasem (Bird Market)

JI Taman

Taman Sari (Water Castle)

To Bantul

Jalan Sosrowijayan area

20

JI Pasar Kembang

Wartel

12

JI Oyonegaran

4 1

JI Maliboro

11 Warpostel

3

16 4 7

JI Sosrowijayan

@

JI MJ Sutoyo

Museum Perjuangan

JI Kol Sugiyono I

15

Parangtritis

JI Tirtodipuran

17 13 7 9

10 2 10 5 9

To 14 5

N

200 metres
200 yards

At the northwest edge of the Alun-alun Lor is the **Museum Sonobudoyo** ① *Tue-Sun 0800-1400, Fri 0800-1200, 7000Rp*. It was established in 1935 as a centre for Javanese culture, and the collection is housed, appropriately, within a traditional Javanese building. It contains a good selection of Indonesian art, largely Javanese, including a collection of *wayang* puppets, but also some Balinese woodcarvings. On the southwest side of the Alun-alun Lor is the **Grand Mosque**, built in Javanese style, with a wooden frame and a tiled roof.

The Kraton of Yogyakarta → *Numbers in brackets relate to key of plan below.*
The Kraton of Yogyakarta was one of three such palaces that came into existence when the kingdom of Mataram was partitioned after the Treaty of Giyanti was signed with the VOC in 1755. It has been described as a city within a city; it not only houses the sultan's palace, but also a maze of shops, markets and private homes supporting many thousands of people. This section only deals with the inner palace; the kraton actually extends much further, 'beginning' 1 km north at the far end of Jalan Malioboro.

The kraton was started in 1756 by the first sultan, Mangkubumi (who became Hamengkubuwono I in 1749), and finished almost 40 years later. The teak wood used to construct the palace came from the sacred forest of Karangkasem on Gunung Kidul.

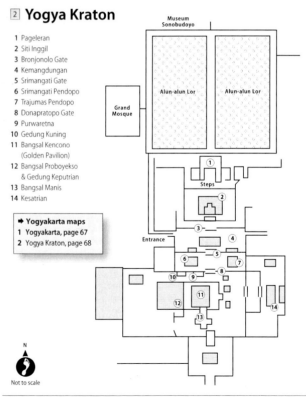

2 Yogya Kraton

1 Pageleran
2 Siti Inggil
3 Bronjonolo Gate
4 Kemangdungan
5 Srimangati Gate
6 Srimangati Pendopo
7 Trajumas Pendopo
8 Donapratopo Gate
9 Purwaretna
10 Gedung Kuning
11 Bangsal Kencono
   (Golden Pavilion)
12 Bangsal Proboyekso
   & Gedung Keputrian
13 Bangsal Manis
14 Kesatrian

➡ **Yogyakarta maps**
1 Yogyakarta, page 67
2 Yogya Kraton, page 68

N
Not to scale

It is largely made up of *pendopo* or open pavilions, enclosed within interconnecting rectangular courtyards. The entire complex is surrounded by high white washed walls.

Facing the Alun-alun Lor is the **Pageleran** (1) ① *Sat-Thu 0830-1330, Fri 0830-1230, 5000Rp*, a large open *pendopo*, originally employed as a waiting place for government officials. Today, this *pendopo* is used for traditional dance and theatrical performances. There are a number of further *pendopo* surrounding this one, containing mediocre displays of regal clothing. The very first classes of the newly created Gajah Mada University were held under these shaded pavilions. To the south of the Pageleran, up some steps, is the **Siti Inggil** (2), meaning 'high ground'. This is the spot where new sultans are crowned. Behind the Siti Inggil is the **Bronjonolo Gate** (3), which is kept closed.

The entrance to the main body of the palace is further south, down Jalan Rotowijayan, on the west side of the Pageleran complex. The first courtyard is the shaded **Kemangdungan** or **Keben** (4), with two small *pendopo*, where the *abdi dalem* or palace servants gather. The 'black' sand that covers most of the ground around the *pendopo* and other buildings in the kraton is from the beaches of the south coast. In this way, it is ensured that the Queen of the South Seas, Nyi Loro Kidul, with whom the sultan is believed to have intimate relations, is present throughout the palace.

The **Srimanganti** (meaning 'to wait for the king') **Gate** (5) leads into a second, rather more impressive, courtyard with two *pendopo* facing each other; the **Srimanganti** (6) to the right and the **Trajumas** (7) to the left. The former was used to receive important guests, while the latter probably served as a court of law. The Srimanganti now contains gongs and other instruments that make up a *gamelan* orchestra. The Trajumas houses palanquins, litters and chairs, as well as a cage in which the sultan's children played. It is said that the children were placed in here, aged eight months, and given a selection of objects – pens, money, books. Whichever took their interest indicated their future careers.

The **Donapratopo Gate** (8), flanked by two *gupala* or *raksasa* statues to protect the palace from evil, leads into the heart of the palace where the sultan and his family had their private quarters. Notice the way that gateways never give direct access to courtyards; they were designed in this way to confuse spirits attempting to make their way into the complex.

Inside this gate, immediately on the right, is the sultan's office, the **Purwaretna** (9). Beyond it is the **Gedung Kuning** (10), an impressive yellow building which continues to be the sultan's private residence. Both are roped-off from the public.

The central and most impressive pavilion in the complex is the **Bangsal Kencono** (11) ① *T0274 373721, Sat-Thu 0830-1330, Sun 0830-1230, admission 12,500Rp, camera 1000Rp extra, guides available with a donation, the palace can be partially closed on official ceremonial days*, or Golden Pavilion. The four teak pillars in the centre represent the four elements. On each is symbolized the three religions of Java: Hinduism (a red motif on the top of the columns), Buddhism (a golden design based on the lotus leaf) and Islam (black and gold letters of the Koran). Unfortunately, because the pavilion is roped off, it is difficult to see the pillars clearly. Behind the Golden Pavilion to the west is the **Bangsal Proboyekso** (12), which contains the armoury, and the **Gedung Keputrian** (12), the residence of the sultan's wives and children, both closed to the public. Immediately to the south of the Golden Pavilion is the **Bangsal Manis** (13), the dining room. **Kemakanan**, a *pendopo* to the south reached through a set of gates, is used for *wayang* performances at the end of Ramadan. To the east, through another gate (to the side of which is a large drum made from the wood of the jackfruit tree) there is another courtyard, the **Kesatrian** (14). The sultan's sons lived here. In the central *pendopo* of this courtyard there is another *gamelan* orchestra on display. Performances are held every Monday and Tuesday, 1000-1200 (the performance is included in the price of the entrance). At the east side of this courtyard is a collection of paintings, the best being by Raden Saleh, a 19th-century court painter who gained a reputation of sorts (and whose grave can be found in Bogor). The photographs of the sultans and their wives are more interesting. North of the Kesatrian is the **Gedung Kopo**, originally the hospital and now a museum housing gifts to the sultans.

Close to the palace, on Jalan Rotowijayan, is the **Museum Kereta Karaton** ① *Tue-Sun 0800-1600, 5000Rp plus 1000Rp for camera*, which houses the royal carriages.

Taman Sari and around

From the palace it is a five- to 10-minute walk to the Taman Sari. Walk south along Jalan Rotowijayan and turn left at the Dewi Srikandi Art Gallery. A number of batik painting galleries are down this road, which leads into Jalan Ngasem and then onto the **Pasar Ngasem** or bird market, an interesting place to wander. Song birds and turtle doves (*Genus Streptopelia*), are highly prized by the Javanese. It is sometimes said that wives take second place to a man's song bird and that they can cost as much as US$20,000.

By picking your way through the Pasar Ngasem it is possible to reach the **Taman Sari** ① *daily 0800-1530, 7000Rp*, which was known to the Dutch as the *waterkasteel* or 'Water Castle', as it is still called. This is a maze of underground passageways, ruins and pools, built as a pleasure garden by the first sultan, Mangkubumi, in 1765, at the same time as the kraton. Surrounded by high walls, it was the sultan's hideaway. He constructed three bathing pools – for his children, his *putri* (girls) and himself. A tower allowed the sultan to watch his 'girls' bathing and to summon them to his company. In addition, there were a series of underwater corridors and even a partly underwater mosque. It is these labyrinths that have led some historians to speculate that it was also built as a retreat in times of war. By climbing the stairs over the entrance gate it is possible to look over the surrounding *kampung*: this was originally an artificial lake, with a large colonnaded pavilion in the middle. Unfortunately, the gardens were damaged during the British attack on Yogya in 1812 and restoration programmes have been rather unsympathetic. It is difficult to imagine the gardens as they were – as a place of contemplation. Most visitors enter the water gardens from Jalan Taman, through the east gate, which leads into the bathing pool area or Umbul Binangun. This small section is the most complete area of the gardens, having been reconstructed in 1971. The gardens fell into disrepair following the death of Hamengkubuwono III, a process which was accelerated by a devastating earthquake in 1865. Much of the garden has no water in it now, which is disappointing.

To the southeast of the kraton and Taman Sari on Jalan Kol Sugiyono is the small **Museum Perjuangan** ① *Tue-Sun 0800-1600, admission by donation*, or the Struggle for Independence Museum. As the name suggests, this commemorates Indonesia's Declaration of Independence on 17 August 1945 and has a less than inspiring collection of historical artefacts. The museum suffered extensive damage during the earthquake of 2006.

Vredeburg Fort and around

① *Tue-Sun 0800-1600, 750Rp plus 3000Rp for camera.*

The Vredeburg Fort lies to the north of the kraton on the east side of Jalan Jend A Yani, near the intersection with Jalan P Senopati. It was built in 1765 by the Dutch as a military barracks. Restored in the late 1980s, the fort has lost what character it may have had. Now a museum, the fortress houses a series of dioramas depicting the history of Yogyakarta. Close by is the **March 1st Monument**, which commemorates the taking of Yogya from the Dutch in 1949 by a band of guerrillas led by (then) Colonel Suharto. The **Beringharjo Market** is set back from Jalan Jend A Yani on the same side of the street and just north of the Vredeburg Fort. A dimly lit mixed market, it is an interesting and colourful place to wander with fruit, vegetables, fish and meat, batik and household goods – all jumbled together and seemingly fighting for air. Locals warn that numerous pickpockets operate here. On the other side of Jalan Jend A Yani is **Margo Mulyo Church**, which dates from 1830.

Across the road from the fort is the **Gedung Agung**, built initially in 1823 and then rebuilt in 1869 after the devastating earthquake of 1865. It was the former home of the Dutch Resident in Yogya and is now a state guesthouse. Queen Elizabeth II of Great Britain, former Prime Minister Nehru of India and Queen Sirikit of Thailand have all stayed here. Between 1946 and 1949, President Sukarno lived in the Gedung Agung, while Yogya was the capital of an emerging independent Indonesia. South of the fort, on Jalan P Senopati, are three impressive **colonial buildings**, the General Post Office (1910), the Bank Indonesia and the Bank Negara Indonesia (1923).

Jalan Malioboro and Jalan Mangkubumi

North from the Vredeburg Fort, Jalan Jend A Yani becomes Jalan Malioboro; this is the tourist heart of Yogya, with shops, restaurants and a smattering of hotels. The town has the largest student population in Indonesia, and in the evenings they congregate along Jalan Malioboro – no doubt for intellectual discussions, as well as eating and music – and stay there till 0400. This has become known as the 'Malioboro culture'. At its north extension, Malioboro becomes Jalan Mangkubumi.

To the west of Jalan Mangkubumi in Tegalrejo is **Sasono Wirotomo**, or the **Diponegoro Museum** ① *Tue-Sun 0900-1300 (regulations state that foreign visitors need a special permit to enter the museum, granted only in Jakarta, ask at the tourist information office in Jakarta for further information)*, a house built on the site of Prince Diponegoro's residence, which was levelled by the Dutch in 1825. The museum contains the prince's memorabilia, including a collection of weapons. At the end of Jalan Malioboro is an **obelisk** or *tugu* that marks the north limit of the kraton. The original *tugu* was erected in 1755, but collapsed; the present structure dates from 1889. Aart van Beek, in his book *Life in the Javanese Kraton*, explains that this was: "the focal point for the Sultan who would sit at an elevated place near the entrance of the palace and meditate by aligning his eyes with the *tugu* and the 3000-m-high Merapi volcano behind, in the distance".

East of the centre

To the east of the town centre, on Jalan Sultan Agung, is **Paku Alam's Palace** ① *Tue, Thu and Sun 0930-1330, 7000Rp*. A small part of the palace in the East Wing is a museum. Further east still, on Jalan Kusumanegara, is the **Gembira Loka Zoo and Amusement Park** ① *daily 0800-1800, 8000Rp*. It contains a reasonable range of Indonesian animals, including the Komodo dragon, orang-utan, tiger and rhinoceros.

Kota Gede ① *admission by voluntary contribution, Fri 1300-1600 for the actual cemetery, but the other areas are open daily, get to the tombs and workshops by taxi or by town bus (bis kota) No 4 or 8 from Jln Jend Sudirman, No 11 from Umbunharjo terminal and No 14 from Jln Prawirotaman*, also known as Sar Gede, lies 5 km to the southeast of Yogya and was the capital of the 16th-century Mataram Kingdom. Nothing remains except for the **tombs** of the rulers of Mataram; in particular, Panembahan Senopati, the founder of the kingdom and his son Krapyak (the father of the famous Sultan Agung). Senopati's son-in-law, Ki Ageng Mangir, is also buried here, his tomb protruding into common ground as he was Senopati's foe. About 100 m from the cemetery is the Watu Gilang, a stone on which Senopati killed Ki Ageng Mangir by smashing his head against it. Walled gardens and ponds containing fish and a yellow turtle, have claimed magical powers ('several hundred years old') and add to the atmosphere. Like the tombs of Imogiri, visitors must wear traditional Javanese dress which can be hired at the entrance (500Rp). Kota Gede is better known for its **silver workshops** which date back to the 17th-century rule of Sultan Agung. Both traditional silver and black (oxydized) silverwork can be purchased.

Taru Martani ① *Mon-Fri 0730-1500, there are English-, Dutch- and German-speaking guides,* is a cigar factory on Jalan Kompil B Suprapto, on the east side of town, where visitors can watch the process of cigar manufacture.

Education capital
The **Indonesian Art Institute (ISI)** is based in Yogyakarta, with faculties of Fine Art, Dance and Music, which partly explains why so much art can be found around town. (The town is the best place to see *wayang* performances and traditional dance.) In recent years it has become a popular town for Indonesian artists to base themselves. On the northern edge of the city is Indonesia's oldest, and one of its most prestigious, universities: **Gadjah Mada University (UGM)**. It was 'founded' in December 1949, when Sultan Hamengkubuwono IX allowed students and their teachers to use the Siti Inggil within the kraton. The campus can be a stimulating place for a stroll, and on Sundays hundreds of students can be seen practising martial arts at the university boulevard between 0700 and 0900, giving the place a very Chinese feeling.

Around Yogyakarta → *For listings, see pages 74-83.*

Hindu and Buddhist monuments, including the largest Buddhist monument in the world, Borobudur (see page 84), the magnificent Hindu temples at Prambanan (see page 88) and the small Hindu temples on the Dieng Plateau can also all be visited on day trips.

Tombs of the Mataram sultans
① *Admission by donation. Agung's tomb is only open Mon 1000-1300, Fri 1330-1630 and Sun 1000-1330, although it is possible to climb up to the site at any time. Get there by bus or colt, 5000Rp. (Buses continue on to Parangtritis from here – see below.) It is a 1-km walk east to the foot of the stairs from Imogiri town (ask for the makam or cemetery). The bus journey is lovely, along a peaceful country road past paddy fields.*
Imogiri, 17 km to the south of Yogya, is the site of the tombs of the Mataram sultans, as well as the rulers of the Surakarta Kingdom. Perhaps the greatest Mataram king, Sultan Agung (reigned 1613-1646), is buried here. He built the cemetery in 1645, preparing a suitably magnificent site for his grave, on a hillside to the south of his court at Kartasura. It is said that he chose this site so that he had a view of the Queen of the South (the sea goddess Nyi Loro Kidul). To reach his **tomb** ① *Sun and Mon 1000-1300, Fri 1300-1600, 1000Rp, directly in front at the top of the stairway,* and those of 23 other royal personages (Surakarta susuhunans to the left, Yogya sultans to the right), the visitor must stagger up 345 steps. Walk behind the tombs to the top of the hill for fine views of the surrounding countryside. Javanese dress, which can be hired at the site, is required to enter the mausoleums. The Yogyakartan equivalent of Chelsea pensioners, with turbans and krisses, make sure correct behaviour is observed at all times. A traditional ceremony involving the filling of four bronze water containers – known as *enceh* – is held in the Javanese month

of Suro; the first month of the year (June). The containers are placed at the gates of the cemetery and are an expression of gratitude to God for the provision of water.

Parangtritis

ⓘ *Regular connections with Yogya's Umbunharjo bus terminal (10,000Rp), either via Kretek along the main road and over the Opak River, or via Imogiri and Celuk. Those staying on Jln Prawirotaman can simply head to Jln Parangritis and flag down any bus heading to Parangritis. To get to Jln Parangritis from town, jump on TransJogja bus 2A and alight at Jln Kol Sugiono. The longer, rougher, trip via Imogiri passes through beautiful rural scenery.*

Parangtritis is a small seaside resort 28 km south of Yogya. It is accessible on a day excursion, although there are a number of places to stay.

Jatijajar Caves

ⓘ *2000Rp, 7 km west of Gombong, turn left; the caves are 13 km off the main road, there are minibuses from Kebumen (50 km) and from Gombong. Gombong is accessible from Yogya, Cilacap and Semarang, among other towns.*

Jatijajar Caves are to be found in the side of a strange ridge of jagged hills, southwest of the small town of Gombong and 157 km west from Yogya. Outside the entrance is a large concrete dinosaur which acts as a spout for the underground spring (bathing pools here). Inside, there are stalactites and stalagmites, springs and theatrical statues of human beings and animals which apparently recount the history of the kingdom of Pahaharan.

Karang Bolong Beach, near to the Jatijajar Caves, is known as a site for collecting bird's nests for the soup of the same name.

Gunung Merapi

ⓘ *It is imperative to take warm clothing (temperatures near the summit can reach zero) and energizing food. Tour operators often fail to stress the need for this kit.*

Gunung Merapi, whose name means 'giving fire', lies 30 km north of Yogya and is possibly the best known of all Java's many volcanoes. It rises to a height of nearly 3000 m and can be seen from the city. Merapi erupted with devastating and fatal force in late 2010 killing over 350 people. Because the volcano is still very active, it is closely watched by Indonesia's Directorate of Vulcanology who have an observatory here. Its first recorded eruption was in AD 1006, when it killed the Hindu king Darmawangsa, covered the island of Java with ash and is believed by scholars to have contributed to the collapse of the Mataram Kingdom.

Merapi erupted in 2006 causing the evacuation of 17,000 people from its flanks. The 2006 eruption occurred just before the deadly earthquake that flattened Bantul, some 50 km to the southwest. The deadly 2010 eruption, the largest eruption since 1870, caused the evacuation of over 350,000 people and caused massive damage to the area.

Climbing Gunung Merapi Most people start from the village of **Selo** (on the north slope), from where it is a four-hour trek up and three hours down. The trail is easy to follow but is steep and narrow in places (especially towards the top, where parts are quite gruelling); robust walking shoes are strongly advised – this is not suitable for the casual stroller. The spectacular views from the summit are best in the morning (0600-0800), which means a very early start, but it's well worth the effort. To see dramatic fireholes, take the path off to the left, about 25 m from the summit. The route passes a ravine before reaching the fireholes – a 10-minute walk. Guides at Selo charge about 100,000Rp and will offer their houses for overnight stays. Tours are not recommended, as the guides urge the group to walk fast, and walking in a group in volcanic cinder can be dusty. At the time of research tourists were climbing from Selo but it is imperative to check the latest before attempting the climb.

Kaliurang → *For listings, see pages 74-83. Phone code: 0293.*

ⓘ *5000Rp admission fee payable at a booth upon entering Kaliurang.*

The mountain resort of **Kaliurang** is 28 km north of Yogya, on the southern slopes of Merapi at just under 1000 m. It is the only point from which you can climb part way up Gunung Merapi and get good views of the lava avalanches. There are facilities at the **Hutan Wisata** (see below) for tennis and swimming, and a **waterfall** ⓘ *admission 500Rp*, near the bus station. Good walks include a 2.5-km trek to Plawangan Seismological Station, with views of the smoking giant (best in the morning, until about 0900-1000). The 'base station' is filled with *warungs* and has an additional entrance charge of 500Rp per person. The Seismological Station and the road leading to it are periodically closed. If this is the case, there is an alternative 2-km walk from the bus station to a belvedere, which overlooks the lava flow resulting from Gunung Merapi's 1994 eruption. There are good views of the volcano on clear days.

Sights

The brilliant **Ullen Sentalu (Museum of Javanese Art and Culture)** ⓘ *T0274 895161, www.ullensentalu.com, Tue-Sun 0900-1530, US$5*, is a wonderful place to learn more about Javanese culture. The lovingly presented displays emphasise the different types of Javanese batik. **Direktorat Vulkanologi (Pos Pengamatan Gunung Merapi)** ⓘ *Jln Cendana 15, T0274 895209, daily 24 hrs*, is the observation centre for volcanic activity on Gunung Merapi, and the staff are happy for tourists to pop in an look at the seismograph and get information about the latest situation. There is a small exhibition with captions in Indonesian detailing recent eruptions, with some grim photographs showing just how dangerous this beautiful mountain can be. **Hutan Wisata (Forest Park)** ⓘ *next to the bus terminal, daily 0800-1600, 500Rp*, is a small forested park that has a couple of decent strolls, allowing for some great views of Merapi.

Yogyakarta listings

For Sleeping and Eating price codes and other relevant information, see pages 9-11.

⊝ Sleeping

Yogyakarta *p65, map p67*
Yogya's different accommodation categories tend to be grouped in particular areas of town. Most of the expensive international-style hotels are to be found either on Jln Malioboro, in the centre of town, or on the road east to the airport (Jln Jend Sudirman). The former are in a convenient position if visitors wish to explore the city on foot from their hotels. Many middle-priced guesthouses are concentrated on Jln Prawirotaman, to the south of the kraton, about 2 km from the city centre (a becak ride away). These are smallish private villas converted into hotels, some with just a handful of rooms, some with small swimming pools. On Jln Prawirotaman, a gaggle of restaurants, shops and tour companies have grown up to service the needs of those staying here. Finally, there is the budget accommodation, which is concentrated on and around Jln Pasar Kembang and Jln Sosrowijayan, close to the train station. There are tour companies, travel agents, restaurants, car and motorcycle hire

outfits, bus booking companies, and currency exchange offices here. See www.yogyes.com for accommodation and special offers.

Jalan Marlioboro and Jalan Dagen
These centrally located hotels are geared towards domestic tourists, and are more upmarket than those available in the Sosrowijayan area, but not as good value as those in the Prawirotaman area.

$$$ Hotel Ibis, Jln Marlioboro, T0274 516974, www.ibishotel.com. Rooms at this 3-star chain hotel are spotless, comfortable and feature cable TV and minibar. More expensive rooms come with bath. The hotel has a spa, pool, fitness centre and restaurant.

$$ Hotel Kombokarno, Jln Dagen 39, T0274 515812. Clean a/c and fan rooms facing a central courtyard with fish pond. More expensive rooms have TV (local channels only), a/c and hot water. Friendly staff.

$$ Hotel Kristina, Jln Dagen 71A, T0274 512076. Popular new place with a good selection of rooms. The standard singles are good value with TV, a/c and hot water.

Jalan Sosrowijyan area
This is prime backpacker territory, with plenty of cheap *losmen*. The area has seen better days and, with accommodation along Jln Prawirotaman becoming markedly cheaper in recent years, this area has lost its edge. However, it is close to all the action on Jln Malioboro and within walking distance of the train station and the major sights.

$$ 1001 Malam Hotel, Sosrowijayan Wetan GT I/57, T0274 515087, www.1001malam hotel.com. Popular place with plenty of Javanese flourishes and pleasant garden to relax in after a hard day pounding the pavements. Each of the 16 rooms has a massive wall painting done by a local artist. Wi-Fi available. Tours organized. One of the better places in the neighbourhood.

$$ Istana Batik Ratna, Jln Pasar Kembang, T0274 587012, www.dianagrouphotel.com/ istanabatik. The slightly overpriced rooms here are clean and come with a/c, TV and

Wi-Fi connection. Bathrooms are new, and the more expensive have baths. 10% discount in low season. Pool.

$$-$ Bladok Losmen, Jln Sosrowijayan 76, T0274 560452. Welcoming place with a good selection of rooms and a brilliant swimming pool with noisy waterfall, perfect for a back massage (they turn it off at 1700 for fear it will disturb guests). Cheaper rooms are small and have squat toilet, but the VIP rooms are huge, with a/c and TV. Breakfast not included. Recommended.

$ Hotel Karunia, Jln Sosrowijayan 78, T0274 566057. Rooms here are clean and spacious with some artwork on the walls. Cheaper rooms have shared bathroom.

$ Monica Hotel, Jln Sosrowijayan, Gang 2 192, T0274 580598. Simple, clean rooms (the more expensive with TV and a/c), set around a pleasant courtyard with a fountain that functions occasionally.

$ Setia Kawan, Jln Sosrowijayan, Gang 2 127, T0274 552271, www.bedhots.com. Down a small alley off the gang, this popular place is covererd in contemporary artwork and has a gallery attached. There's no escape from the art in the bedrooms, which have wonderfully painted walls. Light comes into some rooms through small windows in the ceiling. Rooms are small, but clean. Good homely atmosphere. Wi-Fi available. Recommended.

Jalan Prawirotaman area
A selection of clean and well-managed middle-range accommodation is to be found on Jln Prawirotaman, south of the kraton, making this the best area to stay in. The hotels are the best of their kind in Yogya. The area's single obvious disadvantage is that it is not very central, but the street has numerous restaurants, shops, travel agents, cultural shows and a couple of watering holes nearby.

$$$ Eclipse Hotel, Jln Prawirotaman 35, T0274 380976, www.eclipsehtl.com. This hotel is the slickest on the street with spotless modern rooms, private balcony with pool view, good daily breakfast and Wi-Fi access throughout. The hotel lacks a little character but makes up for that with its creature comforts.

$$ Duta Guest House, Jln Prawirotaman 1 26, T0274 372064, www.dutagardenhotel.com. This well-run hotel has sparkling a/c and fan rooms, with TV and attached bathroom with bath. Pool and fitness centre. Recommended.

$$ Grand Rosela Hotel, Jln Prawirotaman 28, T0274 419191. Recently renovated, this sprawling place has a selection of simple a/c rooms, with attached bath. The suite rooms at the back come with a spacious communal veranda with views of Merapi, and a long balcony behind with views of the hills to the south. There is also a good-sized pool here. This hotel is slightly overpriced given the competition along the street. However, prices seem to drop by 10-20% upon asking.

$$ Kirana, Jln Prawirotaman 1 45, T0274 376600. This place has undergone some loving renovations and is well decorated with Javanese furniture and antiques. Rooms are comfortable, have a/c and are sparkling clean. The rooms out the back near the small garden are peaceful, although have less light than those at the front. Discounts for long stays.

$$ Ministry Of Coffee, Jln Prawirotaman 1 15A, T0274 747 3828, www.ministryofcoffee.com. The tastefully decorated and comfy rooms feature a/c, Wi-Fi and access to a library as well as all the tea and coffee you can manage. Private balconies. Reservations are advisable.

$$ Prambanan Guesthouse, Jln Prawirotaman 14, T0274 376167. Homely guesthouse with a selection of simple fan and a/c rooms kept spotlessly clean. The rooms on the 2nd floor have views over the pool towards Merapi – beautiful in the early morning. Staff are friendly and there is Wi-Fi access throughout.

$$ Venezia Homestay, Jln Tirtodipuran, T0274 374049, www.venezia-homestay.com. Located down a quiet residential street

5 mins' walk from Jln Prawirotaman, this friendly homestay offers some massive rooms in an opulent house. Friendly owners, Wi-Fi access and plenty of spaces to socialise in.

$ Delta Homestay, Jln Prawirotaman 2 597, T0274 747537, www.dutagardenhotel.com. Small, clean and basic fan and a/c rooms. Friendly staff. Pool.

$ Perwita Sari Hotel, Jln Prawirotaman 1 31, T0274 377592, perwitasariguesthouse@yahoo.com. Popular, with gregarious staff. The fan and a/c rooms are a bit dark, but clean. More expensive rooms have hot water. Pool.

$ Via Via Guesthouse, Jln Prawirotaman Mg 3/514A, T0274 374748, www.viaviajogja.com. Located down a small alley off Jln Prawirotaman, this place has simple but clean rooms, each named after an Indonesian island and adorned with artistic photographs. Some of the rooms have outdoor bathrooms, seperated from the world by a double wall of bamboo, which some guests may find a turn off. Breakfast included, nice garden and free Wi-Fi access throughout.

Kaliurang *p74*

There are over 100 places to choose from in Kaliurang, so availabity is never a problem. Many places are used to groups, and sell blocks of rooms, rather than single rooms. It is possible to get a single room at all the places listed here.

$ Hotel Muria, Jln Astamulya, T0274 446 4257. Spacious, clean rooms with TV. Bathrooms have hot water, squat toilet and *mandi*. Fair value for money.

$ Vogel Hostel, Jln Astamulya 76, T0274 895208. There is plenty of charm at this laid-back hostel. The most backpacker savvy place in town, the rooms here are clean and simple. The bungalows at the foot of the garden are filled with bamboo furniture and have amazing views of Merapi early in the morning. Cheaper rooms in the main building have shared bathroom. There are plenty of magazines to browse, and good information about Merapi. Recommended.

🍴 Eating

Yogyakarta *p65, map p67*

Central Javanese cooking uses a lot of sugar, tapped from the *aren* palm which produces 'red' sugar. Typical dishes include *tape* (a sweet dish made from fermented cassava) and *ketan* (sticky rice). Yogya specialities include *ayam goreng* (fried chicken) and *gudeg* (rice, jackfruit, chicken and an egg cooked in a spicy coconut sauce). Head to the stalls outside the batik market on Jln Marlioboro for some good cheap Javanese fare.

Jalan Sosrowijayan area

$ Bedhot Resto, Jln Sosrowijayan, Gang 1 127, T0274 412452. Inviting atmosphere with plenty of artwork, world beats and a large menu of steaks and pastas with a good vegetarian selection. Recommended.

$ Bintang Café, Jln Sosrowijayan 54, T0274 912 7179. Open 0800-2400. Popular place serving good salads, milkshakes, pastas and Indonesian dishes.

$ FM Café, Jln Sosrowijayan 10, T0274 747 8270. Open 0600-0100. Good helpings of standard Western dishes and a few interesting Javanese options for the adventurous. Happy hour 1300-2000, when a large beer goes for 15,000Rp.

Jalan Prawirotaman area

$$ K Meal's, Jln Tirtodipuran 67, T0274 829 0097. French-owned bistro that has taken Yogya by storm with tables filled with gleefully chomping punters. Food stretches from delectable steak with mash to wood fired pizza. Recommended.

$ Café Janur, Jln Prawirotaman 1, T0818 0265 3488. Open 1000-2300. Dutch-owned eatery with plenty of outdoors seating, chilled beers and a range of Dutch food. The *krokets* and french fries with fresh mayonnaise are a sight for sore eyes.

$ Hani's, Jln Prawirotaman 1 14, T0274 669 2244, www.hanisbakery.com. Open 0800-2300. Good breakfasts with freshly made bread, salads and pasta dishes in a modern,

comfortable setting. Free Wi-Fi access and the *Jakarta Post* to browse, make this a good spot to pass a few hours.

$ Ministry Of Coffee, Jln Prawirotaman 1 15A, T0274 747 3828, www.ministryofcoffee. com. Open 0600-2300. A great place to pass time, with table games, free Wi-Fi access and coffee. The spice espresso shake is delicious, and British travellers will be glad to get their hands on the roast beef and mustard salad. The selection of sweets is naughty, with excellent chocolate mousse. Recommended.

$ Tante Lies, Jln Parangritis, T0274 386719. Open 0900-2200. Essentially an overgrown *warung*, the best choices here are the East Javanese dishes, but there are some pseudo-Western and Chinese choices too.

$ Via Via, Jln Prawirotaman 1 30, T0274 386557, www.viaviacafe.com. Open 0730-2300. This funky restaurant has walls festooned with contemporary art, branches in Senegal, Belgium and Argentina and fine music to accompany a meal. The menu features delicious salads, daily Indonesian specials, pastas and good ice cream. Part of the profits go to local charities.

There is also a food court on the 3rd floor of the **Matahari Mall** (1000-2100) offering good portions of clean, cheap local cuisine.

Kaliurang *p74*

$ Amboja, Jln Kaliurang Km 18.7, T0274 660 6904. Tue-Sun 1100-2100. Located 7 km down the road towards Yogya from Kaliurang, this place has its own organic herb garden and specializes in tasty Indonesian fare. The *ayam asam pedas* (chicken cooked in a spicy tamaring sauce) is particularly good. There is also a range of herb- and spice-infused teas and coffees. Recommended.

$ Beukenhof, part of the Ullen Sentalu Museum complex, T0274 895161. Tue-Sun 1300-2100. An absolute gem of a restaurant set in staggeringly attractive gardens with mysterious walls and plenty of leafy shade. The restaurant is set in a colonial villa with a great tropical veranda. The European menu features classics such as *boeuf bourguignon* and pastas, and some Dutch dishes such as *hutspot met klapstuk* (mashed potatoes with beef and sausage in red wine sauce). Locally made Javanese chocolate bars available.

For cheap, simple travellers grub, try the restaurant at the **Vogel Hostel**. **Wisma Joyo** (see Sleeping) cooks up good Javanese fare.

🍸 Bars and clubs

Yogyakarta *p65, map p67*
Café Janur, see Eating. Run by Arnold Schwarzenegger-lookalike Wim, this place is popular with Dutch expats at the weekend and is a friendly place for a beer.

There are fun bars along Jln Parangtritis, including **Made's**, **Rui's**, and the gay-friendly **Banana Café**.

Live music
Bintang Café, Jln Sosrowijayan 54, T0274 912 7179. Open 0800-2400. Yogyakarta's musical cognoscenti descend on this place on Fri and Sat nights for live reggae and rock 'n' roll with occasional performances by well-known Indonesian bands.

🎉 Festivals and events

Yogyakarta *p65, map p67*
Yogya is host to a number of colourful festivals.
End of Ramadan **Grebeg Syawal** (movable). A Muslim celebration, thanking Allah for the end of this month of fasting. The day before is **Lebaran Day**, when the festivities begin with children parading through the streets. The next day, the military do likewise around the town and then a tall tower of groceries is carried through the street and distributed to the people.
Apr/May **Labuhan** (movable – 26th day of 4th Javanese month Bakdomulud; also held in Feb and Jul). Offerings made to the South Sea Goddess, Nyi Loro Kidul. Especially colourful ceremony at Parangtritis, where offerings are floated on a bamboo palanquin and floated on the sea. Similar rituals are held on Mount Merapi and Mount Lawu.

Jun **Tamplak Wajik** (movable), ritual preparing of 'gunungan' or rice mounds in the kraton, to the accompaniment of *gamelan* and chanting to ward off evil spirits. **Grebeg Besar** (movable), a ceremony to celebrate the Muslim offering feast of Idul Adha. At 2000, the 'gunungan' of decorated rice is brought from the inner court of the kraton to the Grand Mosque, where it is blessed and distributed to the people.
Jul **Siraman Pusaka** (movable, 1st month of the Javanese year), ritual cleansing, when the sultan's heirlooms are cleaned. The water used is said to have magical powers. **Anniversary of Bantul** (20th), celebrated with a procession in Paseban Square, Bantul, south Yogyakarta.
Aug **Kraton Festival** (movable), range of events including ancient ritual ceremonies, cultural shows, craft stalls. **Turtle dove singing contest** (2nd week), a national contest for the Hamengkubuwono X trophy, held in the south Alun-alun from 0700. **Saparan Gamping** (movable), held in Ambarketawang Gamping village, 5 km west of Yogya. This ancient festival is held to ensure the safety of the village. Sacrifices are made of life-sized statues of a bride and groom, made of glutinous rice and filled with brown sugar syrup, symbolizing blood.
Sep **Rebo Wekawan** (2nd), held at the crossing of the Opak and the Gajah Wong rivers, where Sultan Agung is alleged to have met the Goddess Nyi Loro Kidul. **Sekaten** (movable – the 5th day of the Javanese month Mulud), a week-long festival honouring the Prophet Mohammed's birthday. The festival starts with a midnight procession of the royal servants (*abdi dalem*), carrying 2 sets of *gamelan* instruments from the kraton to the Grand Mosque. They are placed in opposite ends of the building and played simultaneously. A fair is held before and during Sekatan in the Alun-alun Lor. **Tamplak Wajik** (5th day of Sekaten). Ritual preparation of 'gunungan' (see above), decorated with vegetables, eggs and cakes at the palace, to the accompaniment of a

gamelan orchestra and chanting to ward off evil spirits. **Grebeg Mulud**, a religious festival celebrating the birthday of Mohammad, and the climax of Sekatan. Held on the last day of the festival (12th day of Mulud), it features a parade of the palace guard in the early morning, from the Kemandungan (in the kraton) to the Alun-alun Lor.

⊕ Entertainment

Yogyakarta *p65, map p67*
Up-to-date information on shows can be obtained from the tourist office, travel agents or from hotels. There is a wide choice of performances and venues, with something happening somewhere every night.

Batik art galleries
3 batik painters from Yogya have achieved an international reputation – Affandi, Amri Yahya and Sapto Hudoyo. The **Affandi Gallery** is at Jln Adisucipto 167 (town bus 8) on the banks of the Gajah Wong River. Daily 0900-1600. It lies next to the home of the Indonesian expressionist painter Affandi (1907-1990) and displays work by Affandi and his daughter, Kartika. The **Amri Gallery** is at Jln Gampingan 67 and **Sapto Hudoyo** has a studio on Jln Adisucipto, opposite the airport.

Batik lessons
Available at: **Batik Research Centre**, Jln Kusumanegara 2, plus a good exhibition; **Gapura Batik**, Jln Taman KP 3/177, T0274 377835 (phone to book), 3-day courses for US$35 including materials (near main entrance to Taman Sari); **Lucy Batik**, Jln Sosrowijayan Gang 1; **Via Via**, Jln Prawirotaman, runs day courses.

Gamelan
Performances at the kraton, Mon-Thu 1000-1200.

Ketroprak
Traditional Javanese drama at the auditorium of **RRI Studio Nusantara 2**,

Jln Gejayan 2030, twice a month (see tourist board for details).

Modern art galleries
Cemeti, Jln Ngadisuryan 7A (near the Taman Sari), has changing exhibits of good contemporary Indonesian and Western artists. Tue-Sun 0900-1500.

Ramayana
Open-air performances at **Prambanan**, T0274 496408, held on 'moonlight nights' May-Oct, starting at 1930 and year-round at the **Trimurti Covered Theatre**, 1930-2130. The story is told in 4 episodes over a period of 4 consecutive evenings coinciding with the climax during the full moon (outdoors Jan-Apr, Nov-Dec only, indoors year round). Tickets cost 75,000-200,000Rp, less at the Trimurti. Most agencies in town sell tickets at face value but add on 50,000Rp for transport to and from Prambanan. There are also performances at the **Purawisata Open Theatre (THR)**, Jln Katamso, T0274 375705, daily 2000-2130. Admission 160,000Rp (it's worth it). Good buffet dinner served before the performance (270,000Rp for the ticket and the meal).

Wayang golek
At the kraton on Wed 0930-1330, 12,500Rp.

Wayang kulit
Performances held at the **Museum Sonobudoyo**, Jln Trikora, daily 2000-2200, 20,000Rp; **Sasana Hinggil** (South Palace Square-Alun-alun Selaton), every 2nd Sat of the month, 2100-0500, 12,500Rp; **Gubug Wayang-44**, Kadipaten Kulon, Kp 1/44, is a *wayang kulit* puppet workshop run by Olot Pardjono, who makes puppets for the Museum Sonobudoyo. Ask at the museum for information on when his workshop is open and how to get there.

Wayang orang
At the kraton every Sun, 1000-1200. Javanese poetry can be heard at the

kraton on Fri between 1000-1200. *Gamelan* is performed at the kraton on Mon and Tue 1000-1200.

○ Shopping

Yogyakarta *p65, map p67*

Yogya offers an enormous variety of Indonesian handicrafts, usually cheaper than can be found in Jakarta. Avoid using a guide or becak driver to take you to a shop, as you will be charged more – their cut. There are hustlers everywhere in Yogya; do not be coerced into visiting an 'exhibition' – you will be led down alleyways and forced to purchase something you probably don't want. It is important to bargain hard. The main shopping street, Jln Malioboro, also attracts more than its fair share of 'tricksters', who maintain, for example, that their exhibition of batik paintings is from Jakarta and is in its last day, so prices are good – don't believe a word of it. The west side of Jln Malioboro is lined with stalls selling batik, *wayang, topeng* and woven bags. Best buys are modern batik designs, sarongs and leather goods. However, the quality of some items can be very poor – eg the batik shirts – which may be difficult to see at night.

Batik Yogya is a centre for both batik *tulis* and batik *cap* and it is widely available in lengths (which can be made up into garments) or as ready-made clothes. Many of the shops call themselves cooperatives and have a fixed price list, but it may still be possible to bargain. There are a number of shops along Jln Malioboro. Batik factories are on Jln Tirtodipuran, south of the kraton, where visitors can watch the cloth being produced. Batik paintings are on sale everywhere, with some of the cheapest available within the kraton walls.

Bookshops Periplus, inside Marlioboro Mall, Jln Marlioboro. Daily 0930-2100. With international newspapers, magazines,

bestsellers and guidebooks. **Book Exchange Yogyakarta**, is a good place to swap books (added cost of around 20,000Rp per book). The best shops are in the Sosrowijayan area, notably **Mas** (Jln Sosrowijayan Gang 1, T0813 2842 0359, 0900-2200), and **Boomerang Bookshop** (Jln Sosrowijayan Gang 1, 0800-2100). There are a couple of second-hand bookshops along Jln Prawirotaman, although the selection of titles is quite poor.

Krisses Kris Satria Gallery, Rotowijayan 2/64, T0811 286743. Open 0800-1800. Interesting selection of kriss (a type of dagger). There are a couple of other places on Jln Prawirotaman 2.

Pottery Earthenware is produced in a number of specialist villages around Yogya. Best known is Kasongan, 7 km south of the city, which produces pots, vases and assorted kitchen utensils. Get there by bus towards Bantul; the village is 700 m off the main road.

Silverware In Kota Gede, to the southeast of the city (most shops are to be found along Jln Kemesan). 2 major workshops are: **MD Silver**, T0274 375063, and **Tom's Silver**, T0274 525416. Numerous shops on Jln Prawirotaman. Try making your own ring with **Via Via Tours**, Jln Prawirotaman, 50,000Rp with instruction, and take home your finished article.

Topeng masks Available from stalls along Jln Malioboro and near Taman Sari. **Wayang kulit and wayang golek** Available from roadside stalls along Jln Malioboro. They come in varying qualities. Hard bargaining recommended. **Putro Wayang**, Kampek Ngadisuryan 1 172, T0274 386611, Sat-Thu 0900-1700, Fri 0900-1100, is a small puppet workshop where visitors can observe the creators at work. They have a small range of beautiful leather *wayang kulit* puppets, *wayang golek* puppets and masks.

▲▲ Activities and tours

For visitors without their own transport, one way to see the sights around Yogya is to join a tour. Although it is comparatively easy to get around by public transport, it can mean waiting around. Yogya has many companies offering tours to the sights in and around the city, mainly centred on Jln Prawirotaman.

There are city tours to the kraton, Taman Sari, batik factories, *wayang* performances and Kota Gede silver workshops.

Also out of town tours to Prambanan (US$9, transport only), Borobudur (US$6, transport only), the Dieng Plateau (US$22), Kaliurang, Parangtritis, Solo and Candi Sukuh, Gedung Songo, Gunung Bromo and Gunung Merapi. Taxis can also be commissioned from US$35 for a full day. Check various companies to select the vehicle, time of departure and cost (tours on non-a/c buses are considerably cheaper). Becak drivers will often take visitors for a tour of the city, and know of some good off the beaten track places. Prices start at US$10 for 5 hrs. Watch out for hidden entrance charges either for yourself or for parking your car.

Yogyakarta *p65, map p67*
Tour operators
There are a number of companies around Jln Sosrowijayan and Jln Pasar Kembang, as well as Jln Prawirotaman, who will organize onward travel by *bis malam* and train. Many of the hotels offer similar services.
Annas, Jln Prawirotaman 7, T0274 386556. Ticketing, car and motorbike rental.
Intras Tour, Jln Malioboro 131, T0274 561972, info@intrastour.com. Recommended by the tourist office for ticketing.
Kartika Trekking, Jln Sosrowijayan 8, T0274 562016. Bus, plane and train ticketing as well as tours around the region and beyond.
Via Via, see Eating. Offers excellent tours.

Vista Express, in Natour Garuda Hotel, Jln Malioboro, T0274 563074.
Yogya Rental, Jln Pasar Kembang 85-88, T0274 587648.

Kaliurang *p74*
Vogel Hostel, see Sleeping. Organizes sunrise walks up the flanks of Merapi to see the lava flows. Walks are led by guides that have a great understanding of local fauna, and plenty of stories to keep walkers enthralled. Depart at 0400, return at 0900, US$10 per person (minimum 2 people) including breakfast.

⊖ Transport

Yogyakarta *p65, map p67*
Air
Adisucipto Airport is 8 km east of town, along Jln Adisucipto (aka Jln Solo). Transport to town: **TransJogja** bus 1A runs to Jln Marlioboro from the airport (3000Rp) a taxi is 55,000Rp. (Taxi desk in Arrivals hall.) Domestic departure tax is 35,000Rp; international is 100,000Rp.

Daily connections with **Kuala Lumpur** and **Singapore** on AirAsia and 3 flights a week with **Malaysian Airlines**.

There are plenty of daily flights to **Jakarta** and **Denpasar**, **Bandung** and **Makassar**. Domestic airlines flying out of Yogyakarta include **Garuda**, **Merpati**, **Batavia** and **Lion Air**.

Airline offices Garuda, Hotel Inna, Jln Marlioboro, T0274 483706. **Merpati**, Jln AM Sangaiji, T0274 583478.

Becak
10,000-20,000Rp per trip. Bargaining hard is essential. Jln Prawirotaman to Jln Marlioboro and back should cost no more than 25,000Rp. Drivers are happy to wait for a few hours. Beware of drivers who offer a very good price; they will almost certainly take you to batik or silverware shops.

Bicycle hire
Along Jln Pasar Kembang or Gang 1 or 2, and hotels on Jln Prawirotaman for approximately 20,000Rp per day.

Bus
Local TransJogja buses criss-cross the town (3000Rp); the tourist office sometimes has bus maps available. Minibuses leave from the Terban station on Jln C Simanjuntak, northeast of the train station.

Long distance Yogya is a transport hub and bus services are available to most places. As it is a popular tourist destination, there are also many a/c tourist buses and minibuses. Agents are concentrated in the hotel/*losmen* areas. The Umbunharjo bus station is 4 km southeast of the city centre, at the intersection of Jln Veteran and Jln Kemerdekaan. Fastest services are at night (*bis malam*). Check times at the bus station or at the tourist office on Jln Malioboro. Regular connections with **Jakarta** (9 hrs) and **Bandung** (6 hrs), as well as many other cities and towns. To get to **Solo** (1½-2 hrs), or north to **Semarang** (3½ hrs), it is better to take a local bus, (hail on the main roads). A/c buses along Jln Sosrowijayan (board bus here too) or from Jln Mangkubumi to, for example, **Jakarta** US$20, **Bandung** US$20, **Surabaya** US$15, **Malang** US$15, **Probolinggo**, US$17.50 and **Denpasar** US$25.

Car hire
Self-drive from **Annas** Jln Prawirotaman 7, T0274 386556. Vehicles are in good condition and vary from US$27 to US$38 per day depending on the size of the car; **Yus** T0852 9282 0222, yoes_pnd@yahoo.co.id, is a knowledgeable Yogya-based driver who drives tourists to Pangandaran and can offer tailor-made tours to most places in Java.

Colt
Offices on Jln Diponegoro, west of the Tugu Monument. Door-to-door minibus service offered. **Rahayu**, Jln Diponegoro 9, T0274 561322, is a reputable company. Seats are bookable and pick-up from hotels can be arranged. Regular connections with **Solo** US$2.50, **Jakarta** US$16 and **Surabaya** US$19. **Anna's Travel** on Jln Prawirotaman has a door-to-door service to **Pangandaran** (7-9 hrs, US$25).

Motorbike hire
Along Jln Pasar Kembang and at **Annas** (see above), 35,000-50,000Rp per day depending on bike size and condition. Check brakes, lights and horn before agreeing; bikes are sometimes poorly maintained.

Taxi
The great majority of taxis in the city are now metered. Flagfall and 1st km, 5000Rp. Taxis/cars can be chartered for the day from **Annas** (see above), or for longer trips to Borobudur or Prambanan. Taxis can be ordered, call **Ria Taxi**, T0274 586166, or **Progo Taxi**, T0274 621055.

Train
The railway station is on Jln Pasar Kembang. Regular connections with **Jakarta**'s Gambir station (8 hrs; the Gajayana night train leaves at 2345 and arrives at 0710). Costs depend on class of train (*eksekutif*, US$31.50). A useful connection is the **Fajar Utama Yogya**, which leaves at 0800 and pulls into Jakarta's Pasar Senen at 1601. 5 daily trains to **Bandung** (*eksekutif* US$21, 8 hrs), 7 daily trains to **Surabaya** (*eksekutif* US$16.50,7 hrs). There is 1 daily connection with **Solo** on the **Prambanan Ekspress** from 0535-1905 (9000Rp, 1hr).

To Bali via Gunung Bromo
A popular way to get to Bali includes a night in Cemoro Lawang, Gunung Bromo, before heading onto destinations in Bali including **Lovina** and **Denpasar**. A night's accommodation at the Café Lava is included. Prices start at US$32. Most travel agencies on Jln Sosrowijayan and Jln Prawirotaman sell this.

Kaliurang *p74*
Bus
There are regular buses from **Yogya**'s **Giwangan** bus terminal and colts from **Condong Catur** bus terminal (1½ hrs, 10,000Rp).

● Directory

Yogyakarta *p65, map p67*
Banks There are many banks in Yogya, rates are good and most currencies and types of TC are entertained. Good rates are especially found along Jln Prawirotaman. BNI, near General Post Office, on Jln Senopati. Money changers next to the **Hotel Asia Afrika**, Jln Pasar Kembang 17 and on Jln Prawirotaman. ATMs on Jln Prawirorotaman and Jln Marlioboro, including inside Marlioboro Mall. **Embassies and consulates** France, Jln Sagan 3-1, T0274 566520.

Emergencies Police: Jln Utara, on city ring road, T0274 885494. **Tourist police**: Tourist Information, Jln Malioboro, T0274 566000, for reporting robberies and seeking general information. **Immigration office** Jln Adisucipto Km 10, T0274 486165 (out of town on the road to the airport, close to Ambarrukmo Palace Hotel). **Internet** Queens Internet, Jln Pasar Kembang, T0274 547633, 24 hrs, 7000Rp per hr. 1+1=11, Jln Parangritis, 24 hrs, 5000Rp per hr. **Medical services** Hospitals: PKU Muhammadiyah, Jln KHKA Dahlan 14, T0274 512653. 24 On-Call Doctor, T0274 620091. **Post office** General Post Office, Jln Seno-pati 2. Post Office Jln Pasar Kembang 37 (for international phone calls and faxes).There are also small post offices by the ticket office at the kraton and along Jln Sosrowijayan. **Telephone** Jln Yos Sudarso 9. Open daily, 24 hrs. IDD international calls.

Borobudur and around

The travel business is all too ready to attach a superlative to the most mundane of sights. However, even travellers of a less world-weary age had little doubt, after they set their eyes on this feast of stone, that they were witnessing one of the wonders of the world. The German traveller Johan Scheltema in his 1912 book Monumental Java, wrote that he felt the "fructifying touch of heaven; when tranquil love descends in waves of contentment, unspeakable satisfaction".

Borobudur → *Phone code: 0293. For listings, see pages 92-93.*

Ins and outs

ⓘ *T0293 788266, www.borobudurpark.co.id, daily 0600-1700, ticket office closes at 1630, (tourists must leave the temple by 1720), US$15, student US$8, video/camera free.*

The entry fee does not include a guide but the extra 75,000Rp fee is really worth it. In theory, visitors should wait for a group to accumulate and then be shown round by a guide, however, many people simply explore the *candi* on their own. There is an extra payment for those who wish to get into the temple at 0430, in time for the sunrise. This can be facilitated by the **Manohara Hotel** (see Sleeping, page 92). For guests of the hotel the additional fee is US$17.50, for non-guests it is US$32. Many consider this money well spent, as the temple is unusually quiet and watching the sun come up from here is quite magical.

The best time to visit is early morning before the coaches arrive, although even by 0600 there can be many people here. Some visitors suggest sunset is better as the view is not affected by mist (as it commonly is in the morning). Consider staying the night in Borobudur, to see the sun rise over the monument.

Background

Borobudur was built when the Sailendra Dynasty of Central Java was at the height of its military and artistic powers. Construction of the monument is said to have taken about 75 years, spanning four or five periods from the end of the eighth century to the middle of the ninth century. Consisting of a nine-tiered 'mountain' rising to 34.5 m, Borobudur is decorated with 5 km of superbly executed reliefs – some 1500 in all – ornamented with 500 statues of the Buddha, and constructed of 1,600,000 andesite stones.

The choice of site on the densely populated and fertile valleys of the Progo and Elo rivers seems to have been partially dictated by the need for a massive labour force. Every farmer owed the kings of Sailendra a certain number of days labour each year (labour tax) in return for the physical and spiritual protection of the ruler. Inscriptions from the ninth and tenth centuries indicate that there were several hundred villages in the vicinity of Borobudur. After the rice harvest, a massive labour force of farmers, slaves and others could be assembled to work on the monument. It is unlikely that they would have been resistant to working on the edifice – by so doing they would be accumulating merit and accelerating their progress towards nirvana.

Art historians have also made the point that the location of Borobudur, at the confluence of the Elo and Progo rivers, was probably meant to evoke, as Dumarçay says, "the most sacred confluence of all, that of the Ganga (Ganges) and the Yumna (Yamuna)", in India. Finally, the monument is also close to a hill, just north of Magelang, called Tidar. Although hardly on the scale of the volcanoes that ring the Kedu Plain, this hill – known as the 'Nail of Java' – lies at the geographic centre of Java and has legendary significance. It is said that it was only after Java, which was floating on the sea, had been nailed to the centre of the earth that it became inhabitable.

The design

The temple is made of grey andesite (a volcanic rock), which was not quarried but taken from river beds. Huge boulders are washed down volcano slopes during flood surges, and these were cut to size and transported to the building site. The blocks were linked by double dovetail clamps; no mortar was used. It is thought that the sculpture was done in situ, after the building work had been completed, then covered in stucco and probably painted.

The large base platform was added at a later date and remains something of an enigma. It actually hides a panel of reliefs, known as the 'hidden foot'. Some authorities believe that this series of reliefs was always meant to be hidden, because they depict earthly desires (true of a similar series of panels at Angkor Wat in Cambodia). Other art historians maintain that this is simply too elaborate an explanation and that the base was added as a buttress. Inherent design faults meant that even during initial construction, subsidence was probably already setting in. In 1885 these subterranean panels were uncovered to be photographed, and then covered up again to ensure the stability of the monument.

The monument was planned so that the pilgrim would approach it from the east, along a path that started at Candi Mendut (see page 87). Architecturally, it is horizontal in conception, and in this sense contrasts with the strong verticality of Prambanan. However, architectural values were of less importance than the sculpture, and in a sense the monument was just an easel for the reliefs. Consideration had to be made for the movement of people, and the width of the galleries was dictated by the size of the panel, which had to be seen at a glance. It is evident that some of the reliefs were conceived as narrative 'padding', ensuring that continuity of story line was achieved. To 'read' the panels, start from the east stairway, keeping the monument on your right. This clockwise circumambulation is known as *pradaksina*. It means that while the balustrade or outer reliefs are read from left to right, those on the main inner wall are viewed from right to left. The reliefs were carved so that they are visually more effective when observed in this way.

The symbolism of Borobudur

Symbolically, Borobudur is an embodiment of three concepts: it is, at the same time, a stupa, a replica of the cosmic mountain *Gunung Meru*, and a *mandala* (an instrument to assist meditation). Archaeologists, intent on interpreting the meaning of the monument, have had to contend with the fact that the structure was built over a number of periods spanning three-quarters of a century. As a result, new ideas were superimposed on older ones. In other words, it meant different things, to different people, at different periods.

Nonetheless, it is agreed that Borobudur represents the Buddhist transition from reality, through 10 psychological states, towards the ultimate condition of nirvana – spiritual enlightenment. Ascending the stupa, the pilgrim passes through these states by ascending through 10 levels. The lowest levels (including the hidden layer, of which a portion is visible at the southeast corner) depict the Sphere of Desire (*Kamadhatu*), describing the cause and effect of good and evil. Above this, the five lower quadrangular galleries, with their multitude of reliefs (put end to end they would measure 2.5 km), represent the Sphere of Form (*Rupadhatu*). These are in stark contrast to the bare upper circular terraces with their half-hidden Buddhas within perforated stupas, representing the Sphere of Formlessness (*Arupadhatu*) – nothingness or nirvana.

The reliefs and the statues of the Buddha

The inner (or retaining) wall of the first gallery is 3.5 m high and contains two series of reliefs, one above the other, each of 120 panels. The upper panels relate events in the historic Buddha's life – the *Lalitavistara* – from his birth to the sermon at Benares, while the lower depict his former lives, as told in the *Jataka* tales. The upper and lower reliefs on the balustrades (or outer wall) also relate Jataka stories as well as *Avadanas* – another Buddhist text, relating previous lives of the Bodhisattvas – in the northeast corner. After viewing this first series of reliefs, climb the east stairway – which was only used for ascending – to the next level. The retaining wall of the second gallery holds 128 panels in a single row 3 m high. This, along with the panels on the retaining walls and (some of the) balustrades of the third gallery, tells the story of Sudhana in search of the Highest Wisdom – one of the most important Buddhist texts, otherwise known as *Gandawyuha*. Finally, the retaining wall of the fourth terrace has 72 panels depicting the *Bhadratjari* – a conclusion to the story of Sudhana, during which he vows to follow in the footsteps of Bodhisattva Samantabhadra. In total there are 2700 panels – a prodigious artistic feat, not only in quantity, but also the consistently high quality of the carvings and their composition.

From these enclosed galleries, the monument opens out onto a series of unadorned circular terraces. On each are a number of small stupas (72 in all), diminishing in size upwards from the first to third terrace, pierced with lozenge-shaped openings, each containing a statue of the Buddha.

Including the Buddhas to be found in the niches opening outwards from the balustrades of the square terraces, there are a staggering 504 Buddha images. All are sculpted out of single blocks of stone. They are not representations of earthly beings who have reached nirvana, but transcendental saviours. The figures are strikingly simple, with a line delineating the edge of the robe, tightly-curled locks of hair, a top knot or *usnisa*, and an *urna* – the dot on the forehead. These last two features are distinctive bodily marks of the Buddha. On the square terraces, the symbolic gesture or mudra of the Buddha is different at each compass point: east-facing Buddhas are 'calling the earth to witness' or *bhumisparcamudra* (with right hand pointing down towards the earth); to the west, they are in an attitude of meditation or *dhyanamudra* (hands together in the lap, with palms facing upwards), to the south, they express charity or *varamudra* (right hand resting on the knee); and to the north, the Buddhas express dispelling fear or *abhayamudra* (with the right hand raised). On the upper circular terraces, all the Buddhas are in the same mudra. Each Buddha is slightly different, yet all retain a remarkable serenity.

The main central stupa on the summit contains two empty chambers. There has been some dispute as to whether they ever contained representations of the Buddha. Those who believe that they did not, argue that because this uppermost level denotes nirvana – nothingness – it would have been symbolically correct to have left them empty. For the pilgrim, these top levels were also designed to afford a chance to rest, before beginning the descent to the world of men. Any stairways except the east one could be used to descend.

The decline, fall and restoration of Borobudur

With the shift in power from Central to East Java in the 10th century, Borobudur was abandoned and its ruin hastened by earthquakes. In 1814, Thomas Stamford Raffles appointed HC Cornelis to undertake investigations into the condition of the monument. Minor restoration was carried out intermittently over the next 80 years, but it was not until 1907 that a major reconstruction programme commenced. This was placed under the leadership of Theo Van Erp, and under his guidance much of the top of the monument was dismantled and then rebuilt. Unfortunately, within 15 years the monument was deteriorating once again, and the combined effects of the world depression in the 1930s, the Japanese occupation in the Second World War and then the trauma of independence, meant that it was not until the early 1970s that a team of international archaeologists were able to investigate the state of Borobudur once more. To their horror, they discovered that the condition of the foundations had deteriorated so much that the entire monument was in danger of caving in. In response, UNESCO began a 10-year restoration programme. This comprised dismantling all the square terraces – involving the removal of approximately 1,000,000 pieces of stone. These were then cleaned, while a new concrete foundation was built, incorporating new water channels. The work was finally completed in 1983 and the monument reopened by President Suharto.

Museum

ⓘ *Free with entrance ticket to Borobudur, daily 0600-1700.*

There is a museum close to the monument, which houses an exhibition showing the restoration process undertaken by UNESCO, and some pieces found on site during the excavation and restoration process.

Candis around Borobudur

Candi Pawon ⓘ *daily 0600-1700, 5000Rp (admission fee includes admission to Candi Mendut, don't throw the ticket away)*, was probably built at the same time as Borobudur and is laid out with the same east–west orientation. It may have acted as an ante-room to Borobudur, catering to the worldly interests of pilgrims. Another theory is that it acted as a crematorium. Candi Pawon is also known as 'Candi Dapur', and both words mean kitchen. The unusually small windows may have been this size because they were designed as smoke outlets. The shrine was dedicated to Kuvera, the God of Fortune. The temple sits on a square base and has an empty chamber. The exterior has some fine reliefs of female figures within pillared frames – reminiscent of Indian carvings – while the roof bears tiers of stupas. Among the reliefs are *kalpataru* or wish-granting trees, their branches dripping with jewels, and surrounded by pots of money. Bearded dwarfs over the entrance pour out jewels from sacks. Insensitive and poor restoration at the beginning of the 20th century has made architectural interpretation rather difficult.

Candi Mendut ⓘ *Sun-Mon 0600-1700, 5000Rp (admission fee includes admission to Candi Prawon, don't throw the ticket away),* lies further east still and 3 km from Borobudur. It was built by King Indra in AD 800. It is believed the *candi* was linked to Borobudur by a paved walkway; pilgrims may have congregated at Mendut, rested or meditated at Pawon, and then proceeded to Borobudur. The building was rediscovered in 1836, when the site was being cleared for a coffee plantation. The main body of the building was restored by Van Erp at the beginning of this century, but the roof was left incomplete (it was probably a large stupa). The temple is raised on a high rectangular plinth and consists of a square cella containing three statues. The shrine is approached up a staircase, its balustrade decorated with reliefs depicting scenes from the *jataka* stories. The exterior is elaborately carved with a series of large relief panels of Bodhisattvas. One wall shows the four-armed Tara or Cunda, flanked by devotees, while another depicts Hariti, once a child-eating demon but here shown after her conversion to Buddhism, with children all around her. Atavaka, a flesh-eating ogre, is shown in this panel holding a child's hand and sitting on pots of gold. The standing male figure may be the Bodhisattva Avalokitesvara, whose consort is Cunda. There are also illustrations of classical Indian morality tales – look out for the fable of the tortoise and the two ducks on the left-hand side – and scenes from Buddhist literature. The interior is very impressive. There were originally seven huge stone icons in the niches; three remain. These three were carved from single blocks of stone, which may explain why they have survived. The central Buddha is seated in the unusual European fashion and is flanked by his two reincarnations (Avalokitesvara and Vajrapani). Notice how the feet of both the attendant statues are black from touching by devotees. The images are seated on elaborate thrones backed against the walls but conceived in the round (similar in style to cave paintings found in western Deccan, India).

There are no architectural remains of another, Sivaite, monument called **Candi Banon**, which was once situated near Candi Pawon. Five large sculptures recovered from the site, all examples of the Central Javanese Period, are in the National Museum in Jakarta.

Prambanan Plain and around → *For listings, see pages 92-93.*

ⓘ *Daily 0600-1800, admission to complex US$13, student US$7. Guides will show you around, pointing out the various stories on the reliefs for US$5. Audiovisual show runs for 30 mins, most languages available, 2000Rp.*

The Prambanan Plain was the centre of the powerful 10th-century Mataram Kingdom that vanquished the Sailendra Dynasty – the builders of Borobudur. At the height of its influence, Mataram encompassed both Central and East Java, together with Bali, Lombok, southwest Borneo and south Sulawesi. The magnificent temples that lie scattered over the Prambanan Plain – second only to Borobudur in size and artistic accomplishment – bear testament to the past glories of the kingdom. The village of Prambanan is little more than a way station, with a handful of *warungs*, a number of *losmen* and hotels, a market and a bus stop.

Getting there Take the road south before crossing the Opak River, towards Piyungan, for about 5 km. On the road, just over a bridge on the left-hand side, are steep stone stairs that climb 100 m to the summit of the plateau and to the kraton. Alternatively, it is possible to drive to the top; further on along the main road, a turning to the left leads to **Candi Banyunibo**, a small, attractive, restored Buddhist shrine dating from the ninth century. It is set in a well-kept garden and surrounded by cultivated land. Just before the *candi*, a narrow winding road, negotiable by car and motorbike, leads up to the plateau and Ratu Boko.

Sights

There are six major *candis* on the Prambanan Plain, each with its own artistic character, and all well worth visiting. The account below describes the temples from east to west, travelling from Prambanan village towards Yogya. The Prambanan temple group were restored by the Indonesian Archaeological Service and now stand in a neat, landscaped and well-planned historical park.

Candi Prambanan or **Candi Lara Jonggrang** (Slender Maiden) as it is also known, stands on open ground and can be clearly seen from the road in Prambanan village. This is the principal temple on the Prambanan Plain, and the greatest Hindu monument in Java. In scale, it is similar to Borobudur, the central tower rising almost vertically, over 45 m. Built between AD 900-930, Prambanan was the last great monument of the Central Javanese Period and, again like Borobudur, the architects were attempting to symbolically recreate the cosmic Gunung Meru.

Originally, there were 232 temples at this site. The plan was focused on a square court, with four gates and eight principal temples. The three largest *candis* are dedicated to Brahma (to the south), to Vishnu (to the north) and the central and tallest tower to Siva. They are sometimes known as Candi Siva, Candi Brahma and Candi Vishnu. Facing each is a smaller shrine, dedicated to each of these gods' 'mounts'.

Candi Siva was restored by the Dutch, after a 16th-century earthquake left much of the temple in ruins. It was conceived as a square cell, with portico projections on each face, the porticos being an integral part of the structure. The tower was constructed as six diminishing storeys, each ringed with small stupas, and the whole surmounted by a larger stupa. The tower stands on a plinth with four approach stairways, the largest to the east, each with gate towers imitating the main shrine and edged with similar shaped stupas. At the first level is an open gallery, with fine reliefs on the inside wall depicting the Javanese interpretation of the Hindu epic, the *Ramayana*. The story begins to the left of the east stairway and is read by walking clockwise – known as *pradaksina*. Look out for the *kalpataru* (wishing trees), with parrots above them and guardians in the shape of rabbits, monkeys and geese or *kinaras*. The story continues on the balustrade of Candi Brahma. Each stairway at Candi Siva leads up into four separate rooms. In the east room is a statue of Siva, to the south is the sage Agastya, behind him, to the west, is his son Ganesh, and to the north is his wife Durga. Durga is also sometimes known as Lara Jonggrang, or Slender Maiden, hence the alternative name for Prambanan – Candi Lara Jonggrang.

The name of this monument is linked to the legend of King Boko and his son Bandung Bondowoso. Bandung loved a princess, Lara Jonggrang, who rejected his advances until her father was defeated in battle by King Boko. To save her father's life, Princess Lara agreed to marry Prince Bandung, but only after he had built 1000 temples in a single night. Summoning an army of subterranean genies, Bandung was well on the way to meeting the target when Lara Jonggrang ordered her maids to begin pounding the day's rice. Thinking it was morning, the cocks crowed and the genies retreated back to their underground lair, leaving Bandung one short of his 1000 temples. In an understandable fit of pique he turned her to stone – and became the statue of Durga. For those leaving Yogya by air, there is a mural depicting the legend at Adisucipto Airport.

The two neighbouring *candis* dedicated to Vishnu and Brahma are smaller. They have only one room each and one staircase on the east side, but have equally fine reliefs running round the galleries. On **Candi Vishnu**, the reliefs tell the stories of Krishna, while those on the balustrade of **Candi Brahma** are a continuation of the Ramayana epic which begins on Candi Siva. On the exterior walls of all three shrines can be seen voluptuous *apsaris*. These heavenly nymphs try to seduce gods, ascetics and mortal men; they encourage ascetics to break their vows of chastity and are skilled in the arts.

Opposite these three shrines are the ruins of **three smaller temples**, recently renovated. Each is dedicated to the mount of a Hindu god: facing Candi Siva is Nandi the bull – Siva's mount; facing Candi Vishnu is (probably) Garuda, the mythical bird; and facing Candi Brahma (probably), Hamsa the goose. The magnificent statue of Nandi is the only mount that still survives.

This inner court is contained within a gated outer court. Between the walls are 224 smaller shrines – all miniature versions of the main shrine – further enclosed by a courtyard.

Candis near Candi Prambanan

From Candi Prambanan, it is possible to walk north to the ruined **Candi Lumbung**, under restoration, as well as **Candi Bubrah**. Together with Candi Sewu, they form a loose complex.

Candi Sewu (meaning 'a thousand temples') lies 1 km to the north of Candi Prambanan and was constructed over three periods from AD 778-810. At first, the building was probably a simple square cella, surrounded by four smaller temples, unconnected to the main shrine. Later, they were incorporated into the current cruciform plan, and the surrounding four rows of 240 smaller shrines were also built. These smaller shrines are all square in plan, with a portico in front. The central temple probably contained a bronze statue of the Buddha. The *candi* has been renovated. The complex is guarded by *raksasa* guardians brandishing clubs, placed here to protect the temple from evil spirits.

Two kilometres to the northeast of Candi Prambanan is **Candi Plaosan**, probably built around AD 835, to celebrate the marriage of a princess of the Buddhist Sailendra Dynasty to a member of the court of the Hindu Sanjaya Dynasty. Candi Plaosan consists of two central sanctuaries surrounded by 116 stupas and 58 smaller shrines. The two central shrines were built on two levels with six cellas. Each of the lower cellas may have housed a central bronze Buddha image, flanked by two stone Bodhisattvas (similar to Candi Mendut, page 87). Again, the shrines are guarded by *raksasa*. The monument is currently being restored.

About 2 km to the south of Prambanan village is **Candi Sojiwan**, another Buddhist temple, undergoing restoration.

The ruins of the late ninth-century **Kraton Ratu Boko** occupy a superb position on a plateau, 200 m above the Prambanan Plain, and cover an area of over 15 ha. They are quite clearly signposted off the main road (south), 2 km. Because this was probably a palace (hence the use of kraton in its name), it is thought that the site was chosen for its strong natural defensive position. The hill may also have been spiritually important. Little is known of the palace; it may have been a religious or a secular royal site – or perhaps both. Some authorities have even suggested it was merely a resting centre for pilgrims visiting nearby Prambanan. Inscriptions celebrate the victory of a ruler, and may be related to the supremacy of the (Hindu) Sanjaya Dynasty over the Buddhist Sailendras.

For the visitor, it is difficult to make sense of the ruins – it is a large site, spread out over the hillside and needs some exploring. From the car park area, walk up some steps and then for about 1 km through rice fields. The dominant restored triple ceremonial porch on two levels gives an idea of how impressive the palace must have been. To the north of the porch are the foundations of two buildings, one of which may have been a temple – possibly a cremation temple. Turn south and then east to reach the major part of the site. Many of the ruins here were probably Hindu shrines, and the stone bases held wooden pillars, which supported large *pendopo*, or open-sided pavilions. Beyond the palace was a series of pools and above the whole complex a series of caves.

Candis on the road west to Yogya

About 3 km west of Candi Prambanan and Prambanan village, on the north side of the main road towards Yogya, is **Candi Sari**. This square temple, built around AD 825, is one of the most unusual in the area, consisting of two storeys and with the appearance of a third. With three cellas on each of the two levels and porticos almost like windows, it strongly resembles a house. Interestingly, reliefs at both Borobudur and Prambanan depict buildings of similar design – probably built of wood rather than stone. Some art historians think that the inspiration for the design is derived from engravings on bronze Dongson drums. These were introduced into Indonesia from north Vietnam and date from between the second and fifth century BC. There is an example of just such a drum in the National Museum in Jakarta. It is thought that both the lower and the upper level cellas of the *candi* were used for worship, the latter being reached by a wooden stairway. The exterior is decorated with particularly accomplished carvings of goddesses, Bodhisattvas playing musical instruments, the female Buddhist deity Tara, and male naga-kings. Like Candi Kalasan, the stupas on the roof bear some resemblance to those at Borobudur. Inside there are three shrines, which would originally have housed Buddha images. Nothing remains of the outer buildings or surrounding walls, but it would have been of similar design to Candi Plaosan. The *candi* was restored by the Dutch in 1929 and like Candi Kalasan is surrounded by trees and houses.

A short distance further west, and on the opposite side of the road from Candi Sari, is **Candi Kalasan** – situated just off the road in the midst of rice fields. The temple dates from AD 778, making it one of the oldest *candis* on Java. It is a Buddhist temple dedicated to the Goddess Tara and is thought to have been built either to honour the marriage of a princess of the Sailendra Dynasty, or as the sepulchre for a Sailendra prince's consort. The monument is strongly vertical and built in the form of a Greek cross – contrasting sharply with the squat and square Candi Sambisari. In fact, the plan of the temple was probably altered 12 years after construction. Of the elaborately carved *kalamakaras* on the porticos projecting from each face, only the south example remains intact. They would have originally been carved roughly in stone and then coated with two layers of stucco, the second of which remained pliable just long enough for artists to carve the intricate designs. The four largest of the external niches are empty. The style of the reliefs is similar to Southeast Indian work of the same period. The roof was originally surmounted by a high circular stupa, mounted on an octagonal drum. Above the porticos are smaller stupas, rather similar in design to those at Borobudur. The only remaining Buddha images are to be found in niches towards the top of the structure. The building contains a mixture of Buddhist and Hindu cosmology – once again evidence of Java's religious syncretism. The main cella almost certainly contained a large bronze figure, as the pedestal has been found to have traces of metallic oxide. The side shrines would also have had statues in them, probably figures of the Buddha.

Another 5 km southwest from Candi Kalasan, towards Yogya, is the turn-off for **Candi Sambisari**, 2 km north of the main road. If travelling from Yogya, turn left at the Km 12.5 marker – about 9.5 km out of town. Candi Sambisari, named after the nearby village, sits 6.5 m below ground level, surrounded by a 2-m-high volcanic tuff wall. It has only recently been excavated from under layers of volcanic ash, having been discovered by a farmer in the 1960s. It is believed to have been buried by an eruption of Gunung Merapi during the 14th century and as a result is well preserved. The *candi* was probably built in the early ninth century, and if so, is one of the last temples to be built during the Mataram period. A central square shrine still contains its linga, indicating that this was a Hindu temple dedicated to Siva. There are also smaller boundary lingams surrounding the temple. On the raised gallery, there are fine carvings of Durga (north), Ganesh (east) and Agastya (south). Pillar bases on the terrace indicate that the entire *candi* was once covered by a wooden pavilion.

Borobudur and around listings

For Sleeping and Eating price codes and other relevant information, see pages 9-11.

☐ Sleeping

Borobudur *p84*
Most people visit Borobudur as a day trip from Yogya. However, accommodation is quite well established here and can get fully booked over public holidays. Although large international hotels are attracted to the area, many budget hostels are in demand and, as a result, the standard is generally poor.

$$$$ Amanjiwo, 10-min drive and 30-min walk from Borobudur, T0293 788333, www.amanresorts.com. A gloriously opulent resort. The hotel faces Borobudur and offers early morning trips to the temple to see the sun rise; magical. 35 gorgeous suites set around the reception, each with a terraced area, shaded day bed and private pool. Facilities include restaurant, spa service, bar, library, art gallery and tennis centre. Offers free rental of good mountain bikes to explore the countryside. Exceptional quality of service.

$$$ Manohara Hotel, Borobudur Complex, T0293 788131, www.manoharaborobudur.com. Smart hotel set in well-manicured gardens, fantastic position, a/c rooms in a peaceful location are fairly good value. Guests do not automatically get access to Borobudur before the gates open at 0600 – there's an additional sunrise fee. There are stunning views of the sunrise and sunset over the temple. The room price includes the temple entrance fee.

$$-$ Lotus Guesthouse, Jln Madeng Kamulan 2, T0293 788281. This well-run establishment is a popular choice for backpackers, with fair rooms. The rooms are clean, but some have bars over the windows. Cheaper rooms have squat toilet and *mandi*. The owner is a great source of local knowledge and can arrange trips around the local area including rafting.

$$-$ Pondok Tingal Hostel, Jln Balaputradewa 32 (2 km from the temple towards Yogya), T0293 788145, www.pondoktingal.com. Traditional-style wooden building set around courtyard, clean smart rooms with bathroom, dorm beds also available, room rate includes breakfast.

$ Rajasa, Jln Badrawati 2, T0293 788276, ariswara_sutomo@yahoo.com. On the road to the Amanjiwa, this friendly hotel has gorgeous views of verdant rice paddies, and clean a/c and fan rooms with hot water.

Prambanan Plain and around *p88*
There are a number of *losmen* in Prambanan village. Few people stay here because the *candis* are so easily accessible from either Solo or Yogya, but it may be worth doing so, to enjoy the sunrise and sunset.

$$$ Poeri Devata Resort Hotel, Taman Martani, T0274 496435. Very quiet setting offering lovely views of sunset and rise over Prambanan, separate cottages with fully equipped rooms and al fresco *mandi*. Pool, upstairs open restaurant with views. Recommended.

$$-$ Hotel Prambanan Indah, Jln Candi Sewi 8, T0274 497353. Simple hotel with a variety of rooms, ranging from hotel to dorm beds, all share the same facilities including pool.

❼ Eating

Borobudur *p84*
There are 2 restaurants within the complex, a number around the stall and car park area, and in Borobudur village, although the quality at most places is mediocre and they are poor value.

$$ Saraswati, Jln Pranudyawardini. Has a reasonable restaurant with good set meals.

$$-$ Rajasa, Jln Pranudyawardini. Open 0700-2200. Has a traveller-friendly menu of good curries, seafood dishes and vegetarian options. Recommended.

❀ Festivals and events

Borobudur p84
May Waicak (movable, usually during full moon), celebrates the birth and death of the historic Buddha. The procession starts at Candi Mendut and converges on Borobudur at about 0400, all the monks and nuns carry candles – an impressive sight. However, during daylight hours the area is mobbed with visitors making a visit more stressful than pleasurable.

▲ Activities and tours

Borobudur p84
Cycling
The tour guides in Borobudur offer 2-hr guided rides around the surrounding countryside for 50,000Rp per person (minimum 5 people). Ask at the ticket office for more information.

Elephant treks
Organized through the **Manahora Hotel** (see Sleeping). 2½-hr treks through the surrounding area. Contact the hotel for further information.

Whitewater rafting
Run by **Lotus Guesthouse** (see Sleeping). 9 km of Grade II-III rafting down the Progo.

⊖ Transport

Borobudur p84
Bicycle hire
From some *losmen*/guesthouses (eg **Lotus Guesthouse**). An excellent way to visit Candi Pawon and Candi Mendut.

Bus
Regular connections from **Yogya**'s Jombor Bus Terminal in the northern part of the city or from the street 15,000Rp, 1-2 hrs (ask at your hotel to find out where the bus stops). For those staying on Jln Prawirotaman, the best place is the corner of Jln Parangtritis and Jln May Jend Sutoyo. The buses run along Jln Sugiyono, Jln Sutoyo and Jln Haryono (1½-2 hrs). Note that the last bus back to Yogya leaves at 1700. Leave at 0500 to arrive early and avoid crowds. From the bus station in Borobudur, it is a 500-m walk to the monument. *Bis malam* (night) and *bis cepat* (express) tickets can be booked from the office opposite the market in the village. There are buses to **Yogya**, **Jakarta**, **Bogor** and **Merak** for those in a rush to get to Sumatra.

Taxi
This may be the best option for 3-4 people travelling together – cheaper than a hotel tour and without time restrictions. Hiring a taxi should cost around 225,000Rp from Yogya.

Prambanan Plain and around p88
In order to see the outlying *candis*, it is best to have some form of transport. If on a tour, enquire which *candis* are to be visited, or hire a taxi, minibus or motorbike from Yogya. Horse-drawn carts and minibuses wait at the bus station; they can be persuaded to drive visitors around.

Bus
Regular connections with **Yogya** on the excellent **TransJogya** system. Jump on bus 1A which passes the airport (3000Rp) from Jln Marlioboro (1 hr). First bus leaves at 0600 and then every 20 mins during daylight hours. Connections with **Solo** (1½ hrs).

❸ Directory

Borobudur p84
Banks Bank Rakyat Indonesia, near the entrance gate to Borobudur temple, inside the complex. There is a **BNI** ATM on Jln Medang Kamulan. **Post office** Jln Pramudyawardani 10. **Telephone** Wartel, Jln Pramudyawardani (opposite the market).

Solo (Surakarta) and around

Situated between three of Java's highest volcanoes – Gunung Merapi (2911 m) and Gunung Merbabu (3142 m) to the west, and Gunung Lawu (3265 m) to the east – Surakarta, better known simply as 'Solo', is Central Java's second royal city. The kraton (palace) of the great ancient kingdom of Mataram was moved to Surakarta in the 1670s and the town remained the negara (capital) of the kingdom until 1755, when the VOC divided Mataram into three sultanates: two in Solo and one in Yogya. Although foreigners usually regard Yogya as Java's cultural heart, the Javanese often attach the sobriquet to Surakarta. Solo's motto is 'Berseri' – an acronym for Bersih, Sehat, Rapi, Indah (clean, healthy, neat, beautiful) – and the city has won several awards for being the cleanest in Indonesia.

Solo is more relaxed, smaller and much less touristy than Yogya and has wide tree-lined streets. There are bicycle lanes (on the main east–west road Jalan Slamet Riyadi) that are almost as busy as the main roads. Reflecting the bicycle-friendly character of Solo, many companies run cycling tours of the city. Solo has gained a reputation as a good place to shop; not only is it a centre for the sale of batik, with a large market specializing in nothing else, there is also an 'antiques' market that's worth visiting.

Ins and outs → *Phone code: 0271.*

Getting there

Solo's **Adisumarmo Airport** ① *T0271 780400*, is 10 km northwest of the city and there are connections with Singapore, Java and the outer islands. The **Balapan railway station**, just north of the city centre, has connections with Jakarta, Surabaya and points along the way including Yogya. The **Tirtonadi bus station** is 2 km north of the city centre, and has connections with many Javanese towns as well as destinations in Bali, Lombok and Sumatra. Book night and express bus tickets through hotels, *losmen* and at travel agencies. Local buses regularly leave Yogya for Solo (two hours). ▶▶ *See Transport, page 108.*

Getting around

Cycling is the best way to explore Solo; the city is more bicycle-friendly than just about any other Javanese town. Angkutans and town buses run along set routes. Becaks are useful for short local trips or for charter. It is also worth taking a becak to explore the streets to find some of the interesting colonial houses.

Tourist information

ⓘ *Jln Slamet Riyadi 275, next to the Museum Radya Pustaka, T0271 711435, daily 0800-1600.* The **tourist office** ⓘ *supplies maps and has information on cultural events.* Staff speak English and are very helpful. Tourist information is also available at the bus station (very poor), the railway station and the airport.

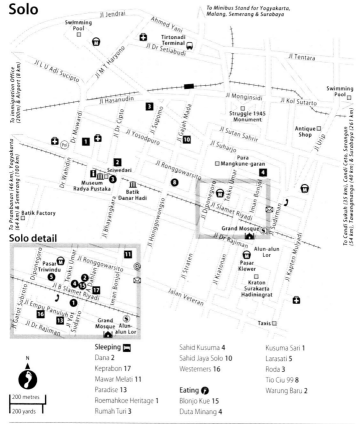

Solo

Sleeping 🛏
Dana **2**
Keprabon **17**
Mawar Melati **11**
Paradise **13**
Roemahkoe Heritage **1**
Rumah Turi **3**

Sahid Kusuma **4**
Sahid Jaya Solo **10**
Westerners **16**

Eating 🍴
Blonjo Kue **15**
Duta Minang **4**

Kusuma Sari **1**
Larasati **5**
Roda **3**
Tio Ciu 99 **8**
Warung Baru **2**

Sights → *For listings, see pages 103-110.*

Kraton Surakarta Hadiningrat

ⓘ *Mon-Thu 0900-1400, Sat-Sun 0900-1500, admission 8000Rp, 2000Rp for camera, all visitors are asked to wear a* samir *(a gold-and-red ribbon) as a mark of respect. Guide obligatory (they are the* abdi dalem *– palace servants).*

The **Kraton Surakarta Hadiningrat**, better known as the **Kasunanan Palace**, is the senior of the city's two kratons and the more impressive. It lies south of the main east–west road, Jalan Slamet Riyadi. Like the kraton in Yogya, the Kasunanan Palace faces north onto a square – the Alun-alun Lor – and follows the same basic design, consisting of a series of courtyards containing open-sided pavilions or *pendopo*. On the west side of the Alun-alun is the **Grand Mosque**, built by Pangkubuwono III in 1750, though substantially embellished since then.

Entering the Kasunanan Palace, the first *pendopo*, the **Pagelaran**, is original, dating from 1745, and is used for public ceremonies. This is where visiting government officials would wait for an audience with the Susuhunan. From here, stairs lead up to the **Siti Inggil** (High Place), the area traditionally used for enthronements. Like Borobudur and Prambanan, the Siti Inggil represents the cosmic mountain Meru, but on a micro-scale. On the Siti Inggil is a large *pendopo*. The fore section of this pavilion was rebuilt in 1915, but the square section towards the rear (known as the **Bangsal Witana**), with its umbrella-shaped roof, is 250 years old.

Visitors are not permitted to enter the main palace compound through the large **Kemandungan Gates**. They must walk back out of the first compound, over a road, past the private entrance to the prince's quarters and an area used to store the royal carriages, through a second gate, to an entrance at the east of the main compound. Near the second gate is a school; this was originally a private school for the royal children but was opened to children of commoners at the time of independence. Walk through one courtyard to reach the large central courtyard, known as the **Plataran**. This shaded area, with its floor of black sand from the south coast, contains the main palace buildings. Much of the prince's private residence was destroyed in a disastrous fire in 1985, but has subsequently been restored. An electrical fault was the alleged cause of the fire, although local belief is that the Susuhunan neglected his duties and provoked the anger of the Goddess Nyi Loro Kidul. Restoration was followed by extensive ceremonies to appease the goddess.

The three *pendopo* on the left are original and are used for *gamelan* performances. Behind them, along the walls of the courtyard, are palanquins once used for transporting princesses around the city. An octagonal tower, the **Panggung Songgobuwono**, survived the fire and was supposedly used by the Susuhunan to communicate with the Goddess Nyi Loro Kidul. Songgobuwono means 'Support of the Universe'.

The main *pendopo*, the **Sasana Sewaka**, is not original – it was restored in 1987 – although the Dutch iron pillars that support it, are. If members of the public are to have an audience with the sultan, they have to walk upon their knees across the *pendopo*: look out for the cleaners, who crouch to sweep the floor. It is used for four ceremonies a year and sacred dances are held here once a year. Behind this *pendopo* is the private residence of the prince, with the **kasatrian** (the sons' quarters) to the right and the **keputren** (the daughters' quarters) to the left. A concrete area to the left was the site of the **Dining Hall**, which burnt to the ground in the fire of 1985 and is awaiting restoration funds.

The guide leads visitors back to the first courtyard, where two sides of the square are a museum, containing an interesting collection of enthronement chairs, small bronze Hindu sculptures and three fine Dutch carriages which are 200-350 years old.

Pura Mangkunegaran

ⓘ *Daily 0900-1400, 10,000Rp, guide obligatory (about 1 hr),* gamelan *performances are held here. Dance and* gamelan *practice is held here every Wed at 1000 and worth seeing.*

The less impressive kraton, Pura Mangkunegaran at the north end of Jalan Diponegoro, is still lived in by the princely family that built it. In 1757, the rebel prince Mas Said established a new royal house here, crowning himself Mangkunegoro I. However, his power was never as great as the Susuhunan, and Mangkunegoro's deference to him is evident in the design of his palace, which faces south towards the Susuhunan's kraton. Much of the original structure has been restored. Built in traditional style, the layout is like other kratons, centred around a *pendopo.*

This central *pendopo* is the **Pendopo Agung** ⓘ *Mon-Sat 0900-1400, Sun 0900-1300,* built in 1810 and one of the largest and most majestic in Java. Note how the ceiling is painted with cosmic symbols. Behind the central *pendopo* is the **Paringgitan,** a large room that houses, among other things, a good collection of antique jewellery and coins of the Majapahit and Mataram periods. In a corridor behind this room are a number of topeng masks. Voyeurs can peer through the windows into the private rooms of the present prince. Next to the ticket office are three fine carriages from London and Holland.

Around Jalan Slamet Riyadi

The small **Museum Radya Pustaka** ⓘ *Tue-Thu 0900-1400, Fri-Sat 0800-1200, 10,000Rp,* is housed in an attractive building on the main road, Jalan Slamet Riyadi, next door to the tourist office. It contains a collection of *wayang kulit, topeng, gamelan* instruments, royal barge figureheads and some Hindu sculptures.

Next door to the museum is **Sriwedari** ⓘ *daily 0800-2200, park entrance on a Sat is 1000Rp, Wayan orang performances Tue-Sat 2000-2200, 3000Rp,* an amusement park. It is also the home of one of the most famous Javanese classical dancing troupes, specializing in *wayang orang.* It is possible to go for a backstage visit to meet the artists and take photos (25,000Rp, ask at the tourist office).

Museum Batik Danar Hadi ⓘ *Jln Slamet Riyadi 261, T0271 714253, daily 0900-1530, 25,000Rp (includes guide),* introduces visitors to the different methods of batik making including wax stamping and handwaxing, and it is possible to see workers producing batik. There is also a display of antique batik and batik from around Asia. Five-day batik courses are available here, but a minimum of 15 people is needed.

Markets

There are several markets in Solo worth visiting. The antiques market, **Pasar Triwindu,** is situated off Jalan Diponegoro, on the right-hand side, walking towards the Pura Mangkunegaran. This is the only authentic flea market in Central Java and is a wonderful place to browse through the piles of goods. There are some good-quality antiques to be found, but time is needed to search them out. Bargaining is essential. **Pasar Klewer,** situated just beyond the west gate of the Alun-alun Lor near the kraton, is a batik-lover's paradise. It is filled with cloth and locally produced batik – a dazzling array of both *cap* and *tulis.* Prices are cheaper than the chain stores, but the market is very busy and first-time visitors may be persuaded into paying more than they should. It's best to go in the mornings, as it starts to wind down after lunch. Again, bargain hard. At the east side of the Alun-alun are a small number of shops and stalls selling fossils, carvings, krisses, puppets and masks. Don't expect to find anything of real quality, though.

Candi Sukuh

ⓘ *Daily 0700-1700, 10,000Rp. Take a bus from Solo's Tirtonadi station on Jln Jend A Yani to Karangpandan (41 km). Or pick up a bus on Jln Ir Sutami travelling east to Karangpandan. From Karangpandan, it is 12 km to Candi Sukuh. Most minibuses travel as far as Ngolrok, from where there are motorbike taxis up on the steep road to the top. From Candi Sukuh there is a well-worn stone path to the mountain resort of Tawangmangu, an easy 1½-2 hrs' hike.*

Candi Sukuh and Candi Ceto, two of the most unusual and stunningly positioned temples in Indonesia, lie to the east of Solo, on the west slopes of Gunung Lawu. Candi Sukuh stands at 910 m above sea level, and was probably built between 1434 and 1449 by the last king of the Majapahit Kingdom, Suhita. This enigmatic *candi* is situated in an area that had long been sacred and dedicated to ancestor-worship. The style is unlike any other temple in Java and has a close resemblance to South American Maya pyramid temples (which led archaeologists to believe, wrongly, that it was of an earlier date). It is built of laterite on three terraces, facing west. A path between narrow stone gates leads up from one terrace to the next, and steep stairs through the body of the main 'pyramid' to a flat summit. There are good views over terraced fields down to the plain below.

The first terrace is approached through a gate from the west, which would have been guarded by *dvarapalas* (temple guardians). The relief carvings on the gate are *candra sangkala*; the elements that make up the picture signify numbers which, in this instance, represent a date ('1359' is equivalent to AD 1437). On the path of the first terrace is a relief of a phallus and vulva: it is said that if a woman's clothes tear on passing this relief, it signifies excessive promiscuity and she must purify herself. The gate to the second terrace is guarded by two more *dvarapalas*. On the terrace are a number of carved stones, including a depiction of two blacksmiths, one standing (probably Ganesh) the other squatting, in front of which is a selection of the weapons they have forged. The third and most sacred terrace is approached through a third gate. There are a number of relief carvings scattered over the terrace. The figures of many are carved in *wayang* form with long arms, and the principal relief depicts the Sudamala story. This story is performed in places where bodies are cremated, in order to ward off curses or to expel evil spirits. Also on the third terrace are standing winged figures (Garuda), giant turtles representing the underworld (strangely similar to the turtle stelae of pagodas in North Vietnam), and carvings of Bima and Kalantaka. It is thought Bima was the most important god worshipped here. A Bima cult became popular among the Javanese elite in the 15th century.

The 'topless' pyramid itself has little decoration on it. It is thought that originally it must have been topped with a wooden structure. A carved phallus was found at the summit; it is now in the National Museum, Jakarta. Although Candi Sukuh is often called Java's 'erotic' temple, the erotic elements are not very prominent: a couple of oversized penises and little else.

Candi Ceto

ⓘ *Daily 0700-1700, 10,000Rp. From Karangpandan via Ngolrok there are minibuses to the village of Kadipekso; from Kadipekso it may be possible to hitch, or catch a motorcycle taxi, the final 2.5 km to the site. Alternatively walk; exhausting at this altitude. There are reportedly some direct bemos from Sukuh to Ceto, making this journey much easier. The easiest way to reach Ceto is to take a tour, see page 108.*

At 1500 m, Candi Ceto is considerably higher than Sukuh and lies 7 km to the north. Fewer people go here as it's harder to get to. It is possible to walk between the two *candis* (about four hours, no obvious trail, but worth it). It was built in 1470 and is the last temple to have been constructed during the Majapahit era. Candi Ceto shows close architectural affinities with the *pura* of Bali, where the Hindu traditions of Majapahit escaped the intrusion of Islam. Getting to the temple is an adventure in itself (although tours do run from Solo and Tawangmangu); the road passes tea estates, steeply terraced fields, and towards the end of the journey seems to climb almost vertically up the mountain. The road ends at the temple.

Candi Ceto is one of the most stunningly positioned temples in Southeast Asia. It has recently been restored and is set on 12 levels. Nine would originally have had narrow open gateways (like those at Sukuh), but only seven of these remain. Pairs of reconstructed wooden pavilions on stone platforms lie to each side of the pathway on the final series of terraces. There is some sculpture (occasionally phallic) and strange stone decorations are set into the ground – again, very reminiscent of Mayan reliefs. For the best views visit the *candi* in the early morning; clouds roll in from mid-morning.

Candi Jabung
ⓘ *Minibuses running east towards Sitabundo will stop at Candi Jabung. The village of Jabung is small and the* candi *rather poorly signposted; it's situated 500 m off the main road, a pleasant walk through fruit groves.*

Candi Jabung lies 26 km east of Probolinggo, about 5 km on from the coastal town of Kraksaan, in the small village of Jabung. It was completed in 1354 and unusually is circular (although the inner cella is square). It was a Buddhist shrine, built as a funerary temple for a Majapahit princess. The finial is now ruined but was probably in the form of a stupa. The *candi* is built of brick and was renovated in 1987 – as too was a smaller *candi* 20 m to the west of the main structure. The *candi* is notable for its finely carved *kala* head. Visitors should sign the visitors' book.

Gunung Bromo → *For listings, see pages 103-110. Phone code: 0335.*

This active volcano stands at 2329 m and is one of the most popular natural sights on Java, lying within the **Bromo-Tengger-Semeru National Park**. The park consists of a range of volcanic mountains, the highest of which (and Java's highest) is Gunung Semeru at 3676 m. Semeru is sometimes also called Gunung Mahameru ('Mountain above the Hindu gods').

At the time of research Gunung Bromo was on high alert due to several eruptions starting in December 2010. In January 2011 an exclusion zone was set up, with authorities recommending that tourists go no closer than 2 km from the caldera. The resulting ash cloud reached heights of 5550 m and prompted several airlines to cancel flights into Bali for a few days. Check the latest with tour operators in Yogya and Bali before setting out for a trip up Bromo.

For many visitors to Indonesia, the trip to Bromo is their most memorable experience: seeing the sun bathe the crater in golden light, picking out the gulleys and ruts in the almost lunar landscape; sipping sweet *kopi manis* after a 0330 start; and feeling the warmth of the sun on your face as the day begins. No wonder the Tenggerese view this area as holy, feeling a need to propitiate the gods. It is hard not to leave feeling the divine hand has helped to mould this inspired landscape.

That's the good experience. But like most good things, there are those who are disappointed. In particular, you may find yourself surrounded by hundreds of other tourists (especially July to August) barking into mobile phones and shattering the calm. It is hard to feel the divine hand in such circumstances. The viewpoint at Gunung Pananjakan also suffers from the curse of over-popularity: it has become a popular stop for package tours from Surabaya. The buses even travel to the crater floor, making this area even more crowded at sunrise and entrenching further unsightly vehicle marks across the sea of sand.

Ins and outs

The **National Park Information Booth** ① *Cemoro Lawang (near Bromo Permai I)*, has a range of photos and maps, and is a good place to gain some information before attempting Gunung Semeru. The best time to visit is during the dry months from May to November. Avoid Indonesian holidays.

Background

The local inhabitants of this area are the Tenggerese people, believed to be descended from the refugees of the Majapahit Kingdom, who fled their lands in AD 928 following the eruption of Gunung Merapi. They embrace the Hindu religion and are the only group of Hindus left on Java today.

Wildlife in the park includes wild pig, Timor deer, barking deer and leopards, as well as an abundance of flying squirrels. You are unlikely to see much wildlife in the Bromo-Tengger Park unless you manage to get off the beaten track and away from all the human and vehicular traffic. Perhaps the most distinctive tree is the cemara, which looks on first glance rather like the familiar conifer. It is, however, no relation and grows above 1400 m on the volcanic ash, where few other trees can establish themselves.

Reaching the crater

From Ngadisari via Probolinggo and Sukapura The easiest access to the park is from the north coast town of Probolinggo, via Sukapura and Ngadisari, and then to Cemoro Lawang on the edge of the caldera. The turning from Probolinggo is well signposted. The road starts in a dead straight line and begins to climb slowly through dense forested gulleys of dipherocarps. The road meanders, precariously at times, past fields of cabbage, onions and chillies. The route becomes steeper and steeper and only first gear seems feasible in the overladen minibuses. After Sukapura, the road becomes yet more precipitous. The National Park begins at the village of Ngadisari. The road narrows through here and continues up to Cemoro Lawang.

On arrival in Ngadisari, it is important to obtain a ticket (50,0000Rp per person) from the **PHKA (Forest Department of Indonesia) booth** ① *T0335 541038, open 24 hrs*, in order to visit the crater's edge. This is the national park entrance fee and the money is used to protect and develop the area. The trip to the caldera is usually undertaken in the early morning, in order to watch the sun rise over the volcanoes. To reach the summit for dawn, an early start from Ngadisari is essential, leaving no later than 0330. It is easiest to travel to Cemoro Lawang (from Ngadisari) on one of the six-seater jeeps, organized by guesthouses in Ngadisari. It takes 20 minutes by road from Ngadisari to the outer crater at Cemoro Lawang, and is another 3-km walk from here to the edge of the crater. Either take a pony (it should cost about 100,000Rp per pony for a 30-minute return trip) or walk for about one hour along a winding path marked by white concrete stakes, through a strange crater landscape of very fine grey sand, known as *Laut Pasir* (Sand Sea). Vegetables and other crops are grown in the sand, and it is surprising that it doesn't just get blown or washed away. It is also possible to walk the entire way, about 5.5 km, from Ngadisari (four to five hours). The final ascent is up 250 concrete steps to a precarious metre-wide ledge, with a vertical drop down into the crater. Aim to reach the summit for sunrise at about 0530. As this is their business, *losmen*-owners will wake visitors up in good time to make the crater edge by sunrise, and are used to arranging transport.

From Tosari via Pasuruan It is also possible to approach the summit from Tosari, on the north slopes of the mountain. The turn-off for Tosari is about 5 km out of Pasaruan, on the road to Probolinggo. Take a minibus from Pasuruan to Tosari (31 km). From Tosari, take an ojek the 3 km to **Wonokitri** (sometimes minibuses continue on to here). Both mountain villages have basic accommodation available. There is a **PHKA** office at Wonokitri, where it is necessary to pay the park entrance fee of 50,000Rp per person. Jeeps and ojeks are available here to take visitors all the way to the summit of Gunung Panajakan (275,000Rp for a jeep). For those who want to walk, it is 5 km from Wonokitri to Simpang Dingklik and then another 4 km up to the summit of Gunung Panajakan. From the summit, a path leads to Cemoro Lawang. Leave before 0400 to see the sunrise over the crater.

From Ngadas via Malang and Tumpang Visitors can also reach Bromo's summit from the west, via Malang, Tumpang and Ngadas. From Tumpang there are bemos to Gubugklakah, and from there it is a 12-km walk to Ngadas. From Ngadas it is a 2.5-km walk to the crater rim at Jemplang, and then another 12 km (three hours) across the crater floor to Bromo and Cemoro Lawang. At Jemplang it is also possible to branch off and climb Gunung Semeru (see below). This walk is much more of a trek and quite demanding, although easy enough for anyone with a reasonable level of fitness.

Equipment
Take warm clothing as it can be very cold before sunrise. A scarf to act as a mask to protect against the sulphurous vapour, and a torch to light the way, can also be useful. Avoid changing camera film at the summit; the thin dust can be harmful to the mechanism.

Trekking
There are several worthwhile treks in the Bromo-Tengger-Semeru National Park. Ask at your hotel/*losmen* for information and (in most cases) a map. It is possible to trek from **Cemoro Lawang** to **Ngadas**, or vice versa; from Ngadas, minibuses run down to Tumpang and from there to Malang. The trek takes four to six hours; guides are available, but the route is well marked. For the best view of Bromo, trek to **Gunung Penanjakan**, 6 km from Cemoro Lawang. This trek is well worth it if you are staying up in Cemera Lawang. The route is easy to follow but torches are a necessity, as is a degree of adventurous spirit. The trek takes about 1½ hours from Cemera, so it is best to leave before 0400 (ignore advice from hostels to leave by 0300, as that then entails a long, cold wait at the top). Take the road opposite the **Cemera Indah** and follow the winding track that turns to gravel and rock. There are white posts leading the way up but these are difficult to spot in the dark. The track is direct until you reach some steps leading up to the right; these steps can be hard to find, but the track comes to a halt and turns back on itself about 25 m after the steps. At the top of the steps a large concrete shelter has been built. This is a great place to watch the sunrise as it is not busy, and only those who have made the effort to walk will be there. Jeeps can be hired for a sunrise trip taking in both Gunung Bromo and Gunung Penanjakan for US$27.50 (to two locations) to US$45 (to four locations) for a group of six people, departing at 0400 and returning at 0830. Enquire at hotels. Alternatively, it is possible but not totally necessary to hire a guide for the walk up Gunung Penanjakan for around US$10-15. There is a **visitor centre** at Cemoro Lawang, not far from **Café Lava** with a range of photographs and maps. It's a good place to obtain information on Gunung Semeru, although it is rarely staffed.

Around Gunung Bromo → *For listings, see pages 103-110.*

Probolingo → *Phone code: 0335.*

Probolinggo is a commercial town that doubles as a Javanese holiday resort. The inhabitants are a mixture of Javanese and Madurese, and most foreign visitors only stop off here en route to Gunung Bromo. Probolinggo is noted for the grapes produced in the surrounding area, and in honour of the fruit the municipal authorities have created a giant bunch, out of concrete, on the main road into town from Pasaruan. It has earned Probolinggo a sobriquet *Kota Anggur* (Grape Town). More enjoyable still is the port, **Pelabuhan Probolinggo**, north from the town centre off Jalan KH Mansyur – about a 1.5-km walk. Brightly coloured boats from all over Indonesia dock, with their cargoes of mostly dry goods. The northern part of town, centred on Jalan Suroyo and the Alun-alun, is the administrative heart of Probolinggo; the portion further east on Jalan P Sudirman is the commercial heart, with the large **Pasar Barde** – a covered market. The **tourist office** faces the bus terminal. It is not a real tourist office, but an advice centre run by several tour companies. We have received complaints about the office and their business practices.

Gunung Semeru

Gunung Semeru, also known as Gunung Mahameru ('Seat of the Gods'), is Java's highest Gunungain and lies 13 km (as the crow flies) to the south of Gunung Bromo. This route is only suitable for more experienced climbers/trekkers; a guide and appropriate equipment are also necessary.

Climbing Gunung Semeru Gunung Semeru can be reached from Cemoro Lawang or, more easily, from Malang. If you also wish to visit Gunung Bromo as well as climb Gunung Semeru, then it is possible to trek four hours across the sea of sand. Guided all-inclusive treks up the the summit of Gunung Semeru start at US$180 for the two-day/one-night trek. Enquire at the **Cemara Indah Hotel**.

The approach from **Malang** starts with a 22-km bemo ride to **Tumpang**, from which it is a further 26-km (1½ hour) bemo ride to **Ngadas**, where *losmen* accommodation is available. A further 2.5 km from Ngadas is **Jemplang** village, which is the arrival point for trekkers coming across the sea of sand from Cemoro Lawang. **Ranu Pani** is 6 km further on, and this is where the PHPA post is located. For safety reasons, climbers must both check in and out at this post. It is possible to get a jeep as far as Ranu Pani, but any further and it's walking all the way to the summit (another 20 km).

Climbers usually spend one night at Ranu Pani, either camping or in **Pak Tasrip's Family Homestay** (**$**, T0334 84887), where there is a small restaurant, baggage storage and camping equipment for hire. From Ranopani, the next stop is **Ranu Kumbolo**. It takes three to four hours to walk the flat 10-km trail. Climbers may replenish their water supplies at the freshwater lake here. At Ranu Kumbolo, there is a camping area and resthouse with cooking facilities (free).

From Ranu Kumbolo, the climb continues to **Kalimati** (4.5 km), passing through savannah – a great area for bird spotting. There is a campsite at Kalimati and a fresh water supply at **Sumbermani** (30 minutes, following the edge of the forest). The next stop is **Arcopodo**, one hour away. This is a popular camping stop for the second night on the mountain. (Some of the soil is unstable.) The climb to the summit of Semeru has to be carefully timed, as toxic gas from the **Jonggring Saloko** crater is dangerously blown around later in the day. It is unsafe to be on the mountain after midday. The heat from the sun also makes the volcanic sand more difficult to walk on. This last climb should therefore commence between 0200 and 0300.

From the summit, on a clear day, there is a fantastic view down into the crater, which emits clouds of steam every 10-15 minutes. Climbers are advised only to attempt Gunung Semeru during the dry season, as sand avalanches and high winds can be a real danger during the wet season. The temperature at the summit ranges from 0-4°C, so come prepared with warm clothing. For more information, enquire at the Malang **PHKA office** ⓘ *Jln Raden Intan 6, T0341 491820*, or at the information centre at Cemoro Lawang.

An interesting walk is to **Widodaren Cave**, halfway up **Gunung Kursi**. It is rarely visited by tourists, but is a regular worshipping site for the local Hindu Tenggerese. There is a spring at the back of the *gua*, which may explain why local people view the site as sacred. To avoid hours of endlessly traversing the sand sea in search of the path leading up to Widodaren, ask for further directions from the park rangers in the visitor's centre or even get them to guide you. It is a 1½-hour walk from Cemoro Lawang.

Madakaripura waterfall
ⓘ *The turn-off for the waterfall is on the main road up to Bromo from Probolinggo, just before Sukapura, hire an ojek or catch a bemo to Lumbang (1½ hrs' drive) after which it is a further 15-min ride to the waterfall.*
There are people on the approach to the 'air terju', who wait to lend visitors umbrellas to shield them from the water cascading down the narrow path through the hillside. Swimming is possible.

Solo (Surakarta) and around listings

For Sleeping and Eating price codes and other relevant information, see pages 9-11.

⊖ Sleeping

Solo *p94, map p95*
$$$$-$$$ Hotel Sahid Jaya Solo, Jln Gajah Mada 82, T0271 644144, www. sahidjayasolo.com. The outfits worn by some of the staff here wouldn't look out of place at a *Star Wars* convention. This 5-star hotel has spotless rooms, that are well decorated featuring TV and minibar. The hotel has a pool and fitness centre with numerous bars and restaurants. Discounts available.
$$$ Hotel Sahid Kusuma, Jln Sugiyopranoto, T0271 646356, www. sahidhotels.com. This hotel is resonant with birdsong and makes for a quiet respite from the busy streets. The standard rooms are set in a dull block but are clean and spacious. The marginally more expensive cabana rooms have a pool view, TV, bath, minibar and are good value. There is a pool,

bar, fitness centre and spa. Efficient staff. Discounts available. Recommended.
$$$ Roemahkoe Heritage, Jln Dr Radjiman 501, T0271 714024, www. roemahkoe.com. Oustanding hotel in the heart of the city. Those that want to revel in olde world charm will love this hotel, originally the pad of a wealthy batik trader. The 16 rooms are comfortable, simple and elegant with crisp white sheets on the bed and access to a relaxing garden. Wi-Fi available. Recommended.
$$$ Rumah Turi, Jln Srigading II No 12 Turisari, T0271 736606, www.rumah-turi. com. Stylish place founded on green principles not far from the town centre. Rooms are comfy and have flatscreen TV and internet access. Friendly staff and a relaxed ambience make this a very pleasant place to stay. Recommended.
$$$-$$ Hotel Dana, Jln Slamet Riyadi 286, T0271 711976, www.hoteldanasolo.com. The horrific concrete car park is in contrast with the tasteful Javanese reception. The cheaper rooms are dark and a little musty,

but feature a TV and clean bathroom. More expensive rooms are brighter and well furnished. Friendly staff, sizeable discounts available.

$ Hotel Keprabon, Jln Ahmad Dahlan 12, T0271 632811. There is art deco style aplenty here, evident in the chairs, facade and beautiful window shutters. Cheap rooms have dirty walls, TV; pricier ones have a/c and hot water.

$ Istana Griya, Jln Ahmad Dahlan 22, T0271 632667, www.istanagriya.tripod. com. The most popular place in town for budget travellers, this hotel has a friendly atmosphere and offers lots of good local information. All rooms only have windows onto a dim corridor. Rooms are colourful, and have attached Western bathrooms. The more expensive rooms have cable TV and hot water. Free tea and coffee all day. Bike hire and internet access available.

$ Mawar Melati, Jln Imam Bonjol 54, T0271 636434. The cheap fan rooms are a little grungy and have dark bathroom with squat toilet. Things improve drastically as you climb the price range, with good-value, clean, spacious rooms with a/c and TV that are great value.

$ Paradise, Jln Empu Panuluh, T0271 652960. This rambling hotel oozes decrepit charm, with antique lamps and old photos of Solo's past. Rooms are shady, and spacious and the a/c ones are surpisingly cheap and feature a bath. There's plenty of outdoor seating and a distinct lack of guests. Tax not included in the room price.

$ The Westerners, Jln Empu Panuluh, T0271 633106. In a friendly family compound, this place has wholesome vibes. Simple fan rooms and attached Western bathrooms with cold-water shower.

Gunung Bromo *p99*
Ngadisari
$$-$ Yoschi's, Jln Wonokerto 1, 2 km before Ngadisari, T0335 541018, www. yoschi.bromosurrounding.com. Owner speaks good English. This is the best place

to stay, some rooms with hot water and showers, attractively furnished and designed with bamboo and *ikat*, the cottages are excellent value, the restaurant serves good dishes using local produce and the *losmen* is a good source of information. Highly recommended.

Sukapura
$$-$ Sangdimur Cottages, Desa Ngepung Sukapura, T0335 581193. The location here is not good for an early morning ascent of the crater, but those who are lazing around the Bromo area and don't like the cold nights will enjoy the relative warmth. Rooms are large and some have lovely views. It's worth paying a bit more for the rooms with hot water.

Tosari
$$$ Bromo Cottages, T0343 571222. Restaurant, hot water, tennis courts, views.

Cemoro Lawang
Hotels can be full during peak season (Jul-Aug). All hostels have their own restaurants. A good place to stay for early morning walks.

$$ Lava View Lodge, T0335 541009, www. globaladventureindonesia.com. Pleasant spacious rooms all come with TV, hot water and a large buffet breakfast. The rooms are in good shape and very clean. Recommended.

$$-$ Café Lava Hostel, T0335 541020, www.globaladventureindonesia.com. This well-run and friendly hotel has the best-value rooms in town, with their superior doubles with TV, hot water and cosy beds trouncing all the other competition. As you slide down the price range, things get rather ordinary.

$$-$ Cemara Indah, T0335 541019, info@ bromotrail.com. The most popular place for foreign visitors, the economy rooms are characterless ice boxes, but the standard rooms are fair value and have attached bathroom and hot water. It is possible to negotiate cheaper rates in low season.

$$-$ Hotel Bromo Permai, T0335 541021. Usually packed with Indonesian tourists and very busy at weekends. The cheapies have shared bathroom and cold water and are poor value. As you go up the price range things improve with hot water, bath and TV. Prices increase at the weekend. Tax is not included.

Camping As the area is a national park, it is possible to camp (40,000Rp). The site is just before the **Lava View Lodge**, 20 m from the lip of the crater. Ask the national park information booth, close to the Bromo Permai I, for more details and about renting equipment. All visitors who wish to camp must report to the **PHKA** post or the Forestry Department, T0852 3236 7281.

Around Gunung Bromo *p102*
Probolinggo
Most people get in and out of Probolinggo as quickly as possible, but there are a few fair options in town.
$ Bromo Permai 2, Jln Panglima Sudirman 327, T0335 422256. This is the first port of call for most tourists needing a place to crash. Rooms are clean and spacious and some come with an attractive garden view. All the a/c and fan rooms have a Western bathroom. The staff here are friendly, and can help with booking train tickets. The reception desk is open 24 hrs. Recommended.
$ Hotel Paramita, Jln Siaman 7, T0335 421535. Not far from the bus station and tucked just off the busy main street, follow the large signposts to find this hotel with clean and spacious a/c and fan rooms.
$ Hotel Ratna, Jln Panglima Sudirman 16, T0335 412597. Decent clean and large a/c and fan rooms.

⊖ Eating

Solo *p94, map p95*
Solo is renowned as a good place to eat and there is certainly no shortage of restaurants and *warungs* to choose from. Solo specialities include *nasi gudeg* (egg, beans, rice, vegetables and coconut sauce), *nasi liwet* (rice cooked in coconut milk and served with a vegetable) and *timlo* (embellished chicken broth). The Yogyanese speciality *gudeg* is also popular here. Most places are closed by 2130.
$$ O Solo Mio, Jln Slamet Riyadi, T0271 664785. Open 1030-2300. Set in a beautifully painted restored shophouse, this authentic Italian restaurant is the best place in town for pizza, pasta and has carafes of Australian red and white wine. There is a monthly special menu, live acoustic music on Thu-Sun and free Wi-Fi access. Recommended.
$ Duta Minang, Jln Slamet Riyadi 66, T0271 648449. 24 hrs. Great place to go for a fix of *nasi Padang*, with excellent *rendang* and plump *percedel* to satisfy a greedy appetite.
$ Kusuma Sari, Jln Slamet Riyadi 111, T0271 656400. Open1000-2100. Popular place with generous helpings of ice cream, and Western fare with a distinctively Indonesian slant.
$ Larasati, Jln Slamet Riyadi 230, T0271 646600. Open 0800-1700. This delightful place serves up local treats such as *nasi asem asem* (beef in a sweet spicy sauce) and *nasi timlo* (chicken soup with vegetables and Javanese sausage) as well as Indonesian favourites such as *nasi goreng* and *gado gado*. Recommended.
$ Ramayana, Jln Imam Bonjol 49, T0271 646643. Open 0800-2100. Plenty of steaks, sizzling hot plates and Chinese and Indonesian favourites are offered. Popular with nearby office workers for lunch.
$ Roda, Jln Slamet Riyadi (next to Radya Pustaka Museum), T0271 734111. Inexpensive and delicious freshly made *dim sum*, and good selection of Chinese cuisine in a friendly outdoor setting.
$ Tio Ciu 99, Jln Slamet Riyadi 244, T0271 644361. Open 1000-2200. Good portions of Chinese favourites such as *Mapo tahu* (tofu in a spicy Sichuan pepper sauce), *sapi lada hitam* (beef in black pepper sauce) and *ayam kungpao* (chicken with chillies and peanuts).

$ Warung Baru, Jln Ahmad Dahlan, T0271 656369. Open 0700-2100. Friendly place with a huge menu of Western dishes, including some good sandwiches with home-made brown bread. This is also a good, clean place to try Javanese dishes including *nasi liwet ayam* and *nasi gudeg*.

Cafés and bakeries
Blonjo Kue, Jln Ahmad Dahlan 7, T0271 634727. 24 hrs. This a/c coffee shop is a great place to escape the heat, enjoy coffees and juices and indulge in cheesecake and their outrageous truffle cake. Recommended.
New Holland Bakery, Jln Slamet Riyadi 151, T0271 632452. Recommended by many locals as the best bakery in the city.
Purimas, Jln Yosodipuro 51, T0271 719120. Open 0700-2100, bakery with good range of well-priced Indonesian sweet breads and Western-style baked goodies.

Foodstalls
There are many *warungs* and food carts to be found around Solo, which vary enormously in quality; 3rd floor of **Matahari** deptartment store at Singosaren Plaza offers a variety of Indonesian food. Fans of *bakso* should try the excellent street stall **Mas Tris**, Jln Honggowongso (south from the intersection with Jln Slamet Riyadi). There's a night market at **Pujasari** (Sriwedari Park), next to the Radya Pustaka Museum on Jln Slamet Riyadi, with Indonesian favourites like *sate* and *nasi ranies*, along with Chinese dishes and seafood include grilled fish and squid. Carts set up along the north side of **Jln Slamet Riyadi** in the afternoon and evening and sell delicious snacks (*jajan* in Javanese). On the south side of town, near Nonongan, *sate* stalls set up in the evenings. There are also stalls near the train station on **Jln Monginsidi. Jln Tuangku Umar** comes alive in the evenings and is a great place to try local Javanese favourites such as *nasi liwet* and *nasi gudeg*. Other street food to keep an eye open for include *intip* (fried

rice crust with Javanese sugar or spices and shaped like a bowl), *srabi notosuman* (rice flour pancakes topped with sweet rice and chocolate or banana) and *wedang jahe* (warm drink made with ginger).

Gunung Bromo *p99*
Most people eat in hotel restaurants (all **$**, 0730-2130). Food in Bromo is nothing exciting. The **Cemara Indah** has a row of picnic benches on the lip of the crater with spectacular views to accompany their good range of Indonesian and Western dishes. **Café Lava Hostel** serves up pastas, fresh juices and good sandwiches in a homely setting. **Hotel Bromo Permai** has an extensive range of Indonsian and Chinese dishes. Other than the hotels, **Warung Sejati**, T0335 541117, 0600-2200, has a range of cheap Indonesian and Javanese dishes.

🍸 Bars and clubs

Solo *p94, map p95*
Most of the hotels have bars that get quite busy at the weekend and close around 0100. **Saraswati Bar**, Jln Slamet Riyadi 272, T0271 724555, has live music Mon-Sat evenings. You can sing karaoke at **Madunggondo Bar** in the Hotel Sahid Kusuma (see Sleeping).

🎉 Festivals and events

Solo *p94, map p95*
Mar/Apr 2-week fair held in the Sriwedari Amusement Park. On the 1st day there's a procession from the King's Palace to Sriwedari, with stalls selling handicrafts.
Jun/Jul Kirab Pusaka Kraton (movable), a traditional ceremony held by the 2 kratons to celebrate the Javanese New Year. A procession of heirlooms, led by a sacred albino buffalo (the *Kyai Slamet*), starts at the Pura Mangkunegaran at 1900 and ends at the Kasunanan Palace at 2400. The ceremony is 250 years old, from the time of Sultan Agung.

Sep Sekaten or Gunungan (movable), a 2-week-long festival prior to Mohammad's birthday. The celebrations begin at midnight, with the procession of 2 sets of ancient and sacred *gamelan* instruments from the kraton to the Grand Mosque. A performance is given on these instruments and at the end of the 2 weeks they are taken back to the Kraton. A fair is held on the Alun-alun Lor in front of the mosque. The closing ceremony is known as *Grebeg Maulud*, when a rice mountain (*gunungan*) is cut up and distributed. The people believe that a small amount of *gunungan* brings prosperity and happiness.

Gunung Bromo *p99*
Feb Karo (movable, according to Tenggerese calendar), held in Ngadisari and Wonokitri to commemorate the creation of Man by Sang Hyang Widi. Tenggerese men perform dances to celebrate the event.
Dec Kasodo (movable, according to Tenggerese calendar). This ceremony is linked to a legend that relates how a princess and her husband pleaded with the gods of the mountain to give them children. Their request was heeded on the condition that their youngest child was sacrificed to the mountain. The couple had 25 children, then finally conceded to the gods' wishes. When the child was thrown into the abyss she chided her parents for not offering her sooner and requested that on the night of the full moon in the month of Kasado, offerings be made to the mountain. The ceremony reaches a climax with a midnight pilgrimage to the crater. Ritual sacrifices of animals and offerings of fruit and vegetables are thrown in to appease the gods.

⚙ Entertainment

Solo *p94, map p95*
Cinema
Multi-screen, the **Studio 123** in the Matahari department store screens some English-language films.

Gamelan
At the **Pura Mangkunegaran** on Sat 1000-1200 and accompanied by dance on Wed at 0900. Admission is included in the entrance fee to the palace. Also at **Sahid Kasuma Hotel**, daily 1700-2000.

Ketoprak
Traditional folk drama performances at the **RRI**, Jln Abdul Rahmna Salleh, T0271 641178, every 4th Tue of the month, 2000-2400.

Wayang kulit
RRI, every 3rd Tue and 3rd Sat of the month, from 0900 to 0500 the next morning.

Wayang orang
At the **Sriwedari Amusement Park** on Jln Slamet Riyadi, Mon-Sat 2000-2300, 3000Rp. **Pura Mangkunegaran** dancing practice, Wed 1000 until finished, free. **STSI**, T0271 647658, has dancing and *gamelan* practice starting at 0900 daily except Fri and Sun, free.

✪ Shopping

Solo *p94, map p95*
Solo has much to offer the shopper, particularly batik and 'antique' curios.

Antiques Pasar Triwindu, off Jln Diponegoro (see page 97). Much of the merchandise is poor quality bric-a-brac, but the odd genuine bargain turns up. Bargaining is essential. There is also a good jumble of an antique shop on **Jln Urip Sumoharjo**, south of Jln Pantisari with some good things (including batik, stamps, old masks, carvings, Buddhas, etc) for those with the time to search).

Batik Classical and modern designs, both *tulis* and *cap*, can be found at the **Pasar Klewer**, situated just beyond the west gate of the Alun-alun Lor, near the kraton. Prices are cheaper than the chain stores, but the market is very busy and bargaining is essential. It is best to go in the mornings, as the market starts to wind down after lunch. **Batik Danar Hadi**, Jln Slamet Riyadi 261, T0271 714326, daily 0900-1530. **Batik Keris**, Jln Yos Sudarso 62, T0271 643292, Sun-Wed 0900-1900, Thu-Sat 0900-2000. Both these shops are great for browsing. Batik Keris has slightly the edge on everyday wearability, and some of their batik shirts are funky. All prices are fixed.

Handicrafts Bedoyo Srimpi, Jln Dr Soepomo (opposite Batik Srimpi); **Pengrajin Wayang Kulit Saimono**, Sogaten RT/02/ RW XV, Pajang Laweyan Surakarta; **Solo Art**, made-to-order tables, chairs, picture frames and even doorstops, good prices, details in Warung Baru Restaurant; **Sriwedari Amusement Park**, Jln Slamet Riyadi; **Usaha Pelajar**, Jln Majapahit 6-10.

Krisses A fine example will cost thousands of dollars. These traditional knives can be bought at **Keris Fauzan**, Kampung Yosoroto RT 28/RW 82, Badran (Bpk Fauzan specializes in Keris production and sale), and also from the stalls at the eastern side of the Alun-alun Utara.

Markets Pasar Besar is on Jln Urip Sumoharjo and is the main market in Solo, excellent for fresh fruit and vegetables.

Supermarket In the basement of the **Matahari** department store, Jln Gatot Subroto, T0271 664711, 0930-2100.

▲▲ Activities and tours

Tour companies, *losmen* and hotels, as well as independent guides, all run cycling tours of Solo, trips to the kraton, batik and *gamelan* factories, *arak* distillers, Prambanan, Sangiran, Candi Sukuh, or to surrounding villages to see rural life and crafts. Prices vary considerably, but for city tours expect to pay around 70,000Rp, and for out-of-town tours around 1000,000Rp, depending on the distance covered.

Highly recommended is Patrick at the **Istana Griya** and the guide from **Warung Baru** (see Eating) also gets good reports. Most tours are 0800-1400. Some *losmen* and homestays will run batik classes, for example the **Istana Griya**, 75,000Rp for a 5-hr lesson including materials.

Solo *p94, map p95*
Tour operators
Mandira Tours, Jln Gadah Mada 77, T0271 654558.
Miki Tours, Jln Yos Sudarso 17, T0271 665352.
Natratour, Jln Gadah Mada 86, T0271 634376, natra@indo.net.id.
Pesona Dunia Tour, Jln Ronggowarsito 82, T0271 651009.
Warung Baru, Jln Ahmad Dahlan 8. Really a restaurant, but this *warung* also runs highly recommended bicycle tours.

Gunung Bromo *p99*
There is an interesting 2-hr guided tour at the **Gunung Bromo Volcanology Centre** that teaches visitors about the seismic activity of Gunung Bromo. Tours can be booked at **Bromo Permai Hotel**, 75,000Rp per person.

Around Gunung Bromo *p102*
Probolinggo
Travel agents here are notorious for charging inflated prices for bus tickets. It seems that people are charged for a return ticket to Bromo and then find that the return vehicle fails to materialize. Avoid this is by only getting buses at the terminal and paying on the bus. Destinations are clearly signposted above the bus lanes on the roof. Queue here until the bus arrives.

⊖ Transport

Solo *p94, map p95*
Air
Solo's **Adisumarmo Airport**, T0271 780400, is 10 km northwest of the city. Taxis are

available for the trip into town (50,000Rp); there is no easy public transport. There are daily flights to **Kuala Lumpur** with AirAsia (www.airasia.com). SilkAir (www. silkair.com) have expensive flights direct to Singapore. If you want to get to **Singapore** cheaply it is better to fly from Jakarta. Domestic flights are only to **Jakarta**. If you want to fly elsewhere, you will have to fly from Yogya.

Aungkutan/becak/bicycle

Angkutan Ply fixed routes around town. The station is close to the intercity bus terminal at Gilingan. **Becak** For short trips around town, bargain hard. **Bicycle** Solo is more bicycle-friendly than just about any other city on Java; cycling is an excellent way to get around town. Hire is available from Istana Griya, Warung Baru and Westerners (see Sleeping). Daily rental is around 20,000Rp for a good mountain bike.

Bus

The Tirtonadi station, T0271 635097, is on Jln Jend A Yani, 2 km north of the city centre. Most bus companies have their offices on Jln Sutan Syahrir or Jln Urip Sumoharjo. Regular *ekonomi* connections with most cities, including **Jakarta**, **Bogor**, **Bandung**, **Malang** (9 hrs), **Surabaya** (6 hrs), **Semarang** and **Denpasar**. Night buses and express buses can be booked through most tour companies and many hotels and *losmen*. They run to most places in Java, and also to **Lovina**, **Lombok/Mataram** and, in Sumatra, to **Padang**, **Medan** and **Bukittinggi**. Companies including Java Baru, Jln Dr Setiabudi 20, T0271 652967.

   Minibus The Gilingan minibus terminal is near to the main Tirtonadi bus terminal; regular a/c door-to-door connections with **Yogya**, US$3, 1½ hrs; **Denpasar**, US$21, 14 hrs; **Bandung**, US$18; and **Jakarta**, US$20. Tickets can be booked at most guesthouses. For **Gunung Bromo**, minibuses run to **Probolinggo** (8 hrs, US$17).

Train

Balapan station is on Jln Monginsidi, T0271 63222. A/c connections with **Jakarta**, 6 daily, 8-12 hrs. The most useful connection is the overnight **Gajanya** departing at 2253 and arriving in Jakarta at 0710 (*eksekutif* US$29). The only a/c daytime connection with Jakarta is on the **Argolawu** departing 0800 and arriving at Gambir at 1617 (*eksekutif* US$24). If travelling to Jakarta, confirm which station your train is heading to, as trains travel to Gambir, Pasar Senen and Jakarta Kota. Gambir station is the most convenient for travellers. To **Surabaya**, 7 a/c trains daily, 7 hrs. To **Bandung**, 5 daily a/c trains (*eksekutif* US$252.50, 8 hrs. The **Prambanan Ekspres** departs Solo 12 times a day for Yogya (1 hr) from 0335 until 1853 (9000Rp).

Around Gunung Bromo *p102*
Probolinggo

Night buses from Bali usually arrive just before sunrise. Travellers are often deposited bleary-eyed at a travel agency and subjected to the hard sell. Avoid this by hopping in a yellow bemo going to the bus terminal (3000Rp), where onward transport can be easily organized independently.

Bemo It is possible to charter a bemo cheaply, haggle for it. Bemos start running at sunrise.

Bus All the bus destinations are written up clearly at the terminal and it is best to deal directly with the bus companies, rather than the tourist office. The Bayuangga bus terminal is on the west side of town, about 5 km from the centre, on the road up to Bromo. Bemos whisk bus passengers into town (3000Rp). Regular connections with **Surabaya**, 2 hrs, 25,000-30,000Rp, **Malang**, 3 hrs, and **Banyuwangi**, 4 hrs, 50,000Rp. Night buses to **Denpasar**, 8 hrs, at least 2 a day at 1200 and 1930, US$15, economy buses are every hour. A/c buses to **Singaraja** (for **Lovina**); **Jakarta**, US$24; **Denpasar**,

Yogya and **Solo**, US$10, are available at regular times. Many buses to Yogya and Solo go via **Surabaya**, adding considerable time to the journey. Check whether it's direct.

Minibus To **Cemoro Lawang**, 2 hrs, 25,000Rp, leave when full (10-15 people). The 1st bus is scheduled to leave at 0700, but there is often a long wait for it to fill up. The last bus to Cemoro Lawang leaves at 1700. It is possible to charter a minibus for the trip for 250,000Rp. Alternatively, hire an ojek for upwards of 75,000Rp, not much fun with a lot of luggage. If you arrive in Probolinggo later than 1600 for **Gunung Bromo**, the only option is to charter a minibus or hire an ojek (around 75,000Rp).

Train The train station is on the main square or Alun-alun, on Jln KH Mansyur, regular *eksekutif* and *bisnis* connections with **Surabaya** and **Banyuwangi**. There is a direct economy-class train to **Yogyakarta**.

⊙ Directory

Solo *p94, map p95*
Banks Bank BCA, Jln Slamet Riyadi 7. Bank Rakyat Indonesia, Jln Slamet Riyadi 236. Danamon, Jln Dr Rajiman 18. Golden Money Changer, Jln Yos Sudarso 1. Lippo Bank, Jln Slamet Riyadi 136.

Standard Chartered, Jln Slamet Riyadi 136. There are plenty of ATMs along Jln Slamet Riyadi. **Emergencies** Police Station Jln Adisucipto 52, T0271 714352. **Immigration** Jln Laksda Adisucipto 8, T0271 712649. **Internet** Aloha in Sahid Kusuma Hotel (see Sleeping), 4000Rp per hr. Y Online, Jln Gajah Mada 132, 6000Rp per hr. Istana Griya (see Sleeping), 6000Rp per hr. **Medical services** Hospital Kasih Ibu, Jln Slamet Riyadi 404, T0271 744422, most doctors here speak English. **Post office** Jln Jend Sudirman 8, Jln Ronggo Warsite. **Telephone** Jln Mayor Kusmanto 1 (24 hrs). Wartel, Jln Slamet Riyadi 275A (at intersection with Jln Prof Dr Sutomo).

Gunung Bromo *p99*
Banks Bank Rakyat Indonesia, Sukapura. Guesthouses at Ngadisari and Cemoro Lawang change money at poor rates. There is a BNI ATM in Cemoro Lawang that accepts Visa and MasterCard. **Post office** In Sukapura.

Around Gunung Bromo *p102*
Probolinggo
Banks Bank Central Asia, Jln Suroyo. Bank Rakyat Indonesia, Jln Suroyo. BNI, Jln Suroyo. **Post office** Jln Suroyo 33. **Telephone** Wartel, Jln Jend A Yani.